104 - solidarity
111 - live in world, not above
131 - in the bright sun of God's love, we start to see our shadow
135 - loved admission of sin, not circumlocution

145 - no one has a "lock" on God
146 - God in every person's life

A Big Heart Open to God

A BIG HEART OPEN TO GOD

A Conversation with
Pope Francis

HarperOne
An Imprint of HarperCollins*Publishers*

America

HarperOne

America

A BIG HEART OPEN TO GOD: *A Conversation with Pope Francis*. Copyright © 2013 by America Press. All rights reserved. Printed in the United States of America. No part of this book may be used or reproduced in any manner whatsoever without written permission except in the case of brief quotations embodied in critical articles and reviews. For information address HarperCollins Publishers, 10 East 53rd Street, New York, NY 10022.

HarperCollins books may be purchased for educational, business, or sales promotional use. For information please e-mail the Special Markets Department at SPsales@harpercollins.com.

HarperCollins website: http://www.harpercollins.com

HarperCollins®, ██®, and HarperOne™ are trademarks of HarperCollins Publishers.

America Press
www.americamagazine.org

FIRST EDITION

Library of Congress Cataloging-in-Publication Data is available upon request.

ISBN 978–0–06–233377–3

13 14 15 16 17 RRD(C) 10 9 8 7 6 5 4 3 2 1

Contents

Foreword

Matt Malone, SJ

ORGANIZATIONS AS OLD as *America* rarely do anything completely unprecedented. For every "new" idea, there is a pretty good chance it has been done before, in one way or another, during the course of 104 years of weekly publishing. This interview in *America*, however, is truly a first.

Although we have always been committed, "on a wide and varied field of subjects," as one of my predecessors put it, "to the principles enunciated by the popes, the Vicars of Christ, and found in the major statements of the American hierarchy," *America* has never before been primarily responsible for conveying the words of a pope to an American audience. The fact that the current pope is a Jesuit is not irrelevant, of course, and neither is the fact that this interview is being simultaneously published by our fellow Jesuit journals in the world's other major languages.

The situation is so unusual, however, that it might be helpful to know how it came about. As with a lot of things, it began with an innocent, offhand remark. James Martin, SJ, *America*'s editor at large, and I were catching up in my office a few weeks after the election of Pope Francis. We were talking generally about our editorial approach to the new papacy when Father Martin said, "Why don't we try to interview the pope?" I gave it three seconds of thought and said, "Yes, why not?"

An interview seemed unlikely and would be unprecedented, but we had just lived through six weeks of unlikely and unprecedented events. We briefly discussed how to approach the matter and started to ask around, conferring with Jesuit colleagues in Washington, D.C., and Rome. They all suggested that we contact Federico Lombardi, SJ, the pope's spokesperson. Father Lombardi responded with his customary alacrity and aplomb and told us that in general the pope does not like to do interviews, but that perhaps he could ask the pope our questions during a press conference and that could be a kind of "interview."

Around this time, we learned that our colleagues at *La Civiltà Cattolica,* the Jesuit journal edited in Rome, were now also interested in conducting an interview. We concluded that their proximity to the pope, as well as the fact that all content in *Civiltà* must be preapproved by the Vatican, made them the ideal partner. Antonio Spadaro, SJ, of *Civiltà*, then approached Father Lombardi on behalf of both of our journals, and Pope Francis consented to the interview.

At the annual meeting of the editors of major Jesuit journals in Lisbon in late spring, the decision was made to include the Jesuit journals from the other major language groups. We also settled on a format. The editors of each of the journals would submit questions to Father Spadaro, who would organize and collate them and then pose them to the pope in an in-person interview. Once Father Spadaro had transcribed the interview and edited it for clarity and length, he personally reviewed the text with the pope, who approved it for publication. *America* then commissioned a team to translate the text into English. And the rest, as they say, is history.

I leave it to you to judge the pope's remarks in these pages, but I would like to suggest one way of reading the interview. Other popes have given interviews, of course, and while they have been insightful and often spirited, they have also been didactic and formal. I suspect that this interview, along with the pope's extended remarks on the return trip from Rio de Janeiro last July, represent a new genre of papal communication, one that is fraternal rather than paternal. A spirit of generosity, humility, and, dare I say, deep affection is evident in these pages. To put it another way, there is no hint here of the monarchical, preconciliar papacy. Pope Francis speaks to us as our brother; his *we* actually means "we," not "I."

Matt Malone, SJ, *is editor in chief of* America.

A Big Heart
Open to God

The Exclusive Interview
with Pope Francis

THIS INTERVIEW WITH Pope Francis took place over the course of three meetings during August 2013 in Rome. The interview was conducted in person by Antonio Spadaro, SJ, editor in chief of *La Civiltà Cattolica,* the Italian Jesuit journal. Father Spadaro conducted the interview on behalf of *La Civiltà Cattolica, America,* and several other major Jesuit journals around the world. The editorial teams at each of the journals prepared questions and sent them to Father Spadaro, who then organized and consolidated them. The interview was conducted in Italian. After the Italian text was officially approved, *America* commissioned a team of five independent experts to translate it into English: Massimo Faggioli, Sarah Christopher Faggioli, Dominic Robinson, SJ, Patrick J. Howell, SJ, and Griffin Oleynick. *America* is solely responsible for the accuracy of this translation.

Introduction

IT IS MONDAY, August 19, 2013. I have an appointment with Pope Francis at 10 A.M. in Santa Marta. I, however, inherited from my father the habit of arriving early for everything. The people who welcome me tell me to make myself comfortable in one of the parlors. I do not have to wait for long, and after a few minutes I am brought over to the lift. This short wait gave me the opportunity to remember the meeting in Lisbon of the editors of a number of journals of the Society of Jesus, at which the proposal emerged to publish jointly an interview with the pope. I had a discussion with the other editors, during which we proposed some questions that would express everyone's interests. I emerge from the lift, and I see the pope already waiting for me at the door. In meeting him here, I had the pleasant impression that I was not crossing any threshold.

I enter his room, and the pope invites me to sit in his easy chair. He himself sits on a chair that is higher and stiffer because of his back problems. The setting is simple, austere. The workspace occupied by the desk is small. I am impressed not only by the simplicity of the furniture, but also by the objects in the room. There are only a few. These include an icon of St. Francis, a statue of Our Lady of Luján (patron saint of Argentina), a crucifix, and a statue of St. Joseph sleeping, very similar to the one which I had seen in his office at the Colegio Máximo de San Miguel, where he was rector and also provincial superior. The spirituality of Jorge Mario Bergoglio is not made of "harmonized energies," as he would call them, but of human faces: Christ, St. Francis, St. Joseph, and Mary.

The pope welcomes me with that smile that has already traveled all around the world, that same smile that opens hearts. We begin speaking about many things, but above all about his trip to Brazil. The pope considers it a true grace.

I ask him if he has had time to rest. He tells me that yes, he is doing well, but above all that World Youth Day was for him a "mystery." He says that he is not used to talking to so many people: "I manage to look at individual persons, one at a time, to enter into personal contact with whomever I have in front of me. I'm not used to the masses."

I tell him that it is true, that people notice it, and that it makes a big impression on everyone. You can tell that whenever he is among a crowd of people his eyes actually rest on individual persons. Then the television cameras project the images, and everyone can see them. This way he can feel free to remain in direct contact, at least with his eyes, with the individuals he has in front of him. To me, he seems happy about this: that he can be who he is, that he does not have to alter his ordinary way of communicating with others, even when he is in front of millions of people, as happened on the beach at Copacabana.

Before I switch on the voice recorder we also talk about other things. Commenting on one of my own publications, he tells me that the two contemporary French thinkers that he holds dear are Henri de Lubac, SJ, and Michel de Certeau, SJ. I also speak to him about more personal matters. He too speaks to me on a personal level, in particular about his election to the pontificate. He tells me that when he began to realize that he might be elected, on Wednesday, March 13, during lunch, he felt a deep and inexplicable peace and interior consolation come over him along with a great darkness, a deep obscurity about everything else. And those feelings accompanied him until his election later that day.

Actually I would have liked to continue speaking with him in this very personal manner for much longer, but I take up my papers filled with questions that I had written down before, and I turn on the voice recorder. First of all I thank him on behalf of all the editors of the various Jesuit magazines that will publish this interview.

Just a bit before the audience that the pope granted on June 14 to the Jesuits of *La Civiltà Cattolica*, the pope had spoken to me about his great difficulty in giving interviews. He had told me that he prefers to think carefully rather than give quick responses to on-the-spot interviews. He feels that the right answers come to him after having already given his initial response. "I did not recognize myself when I responded to the journalists asking me questions on the return flight from Rio de Janeiro," he tells me. But it is true: many times in this interview the pope interrupted what he was saying in response to a question several times in order to add something to an earlier response. Talking with Pope Francis is a kind of volcanic flow of ideas that are bound up with each other. Even taking notes gives me an uncomfortable feeling, as if I were trying to suppress a surging spring of dialogue. It is clear that Pope Francis is more used to having conversations than to giving lectures.

Who Is
Jorge Mario Bergoglio?

I HAVE THE first question ready, but then I decide not to follow the script that I had prepared for myself, and I ask him point-blank: "Who is Jorge Mario Bergoglio?"

The pope stares at me in silence.

I ask him if this is a question that I am allowed to ask.

He nods that it is, and he tells me: "I do not know what might be the most fitting description. . . . I am a sinner. This is the most accurate definition. It is not a figure of speech, a literary genre. I am a sinner."

The pope continues to reflect and concentrate, as if he did not expect this question, as if he were forced to reflect further.

"Yes, perhaps I can say that I am a bit astute, that I can adapt to circumstances, but it is also true that I am a bit naïve. Yes, but the best summary, the one that comes more from the inside and I feel most true is this: I am a sinner whom the Lord has looked upon." And he repeats, "I am one who is looked upon by the Lord. I always felt my motto, *Miserando atque eligendo* [By Having Mercy and by Choosing Him], was very true for me."

The motto is taken from the *Homilies* of Bede the Venerable, who writes in his comments on the Gospel story of the calling of Matthew: "Jesus saw a publican, and since he looked at him with feelings of love and chose him, he said to him, 'Follow me.'" The pope adds, "I think the Latin gerund *miserando* is impossible to translate in both Italian and Spanish. I like to translate it with another gerund that does not exist: *misericordiando* [mercy-ing]."

Pope Francis continues his reflection and tells me, in a change of topic that I do not immediately understand, "I do not know Rome well. I know a few things. These include the Basilica of St. Mary Major; I always used to go there."

I laugh and I tell him, "We all understood that very well, Holy Father!"

"Right, yes," the pope continues. "I know St. Mary Major, St. Peter's . . . but when I had to come to Rome, I always stayed in [the neighborhood of] Via della Scrofa. From there I often visited the Church of St. Louis of France, and I went there to contemplate the painting of *The Calling of St. Matthew,* by Caravaggio."

I begin to intuit what the pope wants to tell me.

"That finger of Jesus, pointing at Matthew. That's me. I feel like him. Like Matthew." Here the pope becomes determined, as if he had finally found the image he was looking for. "It is the gesture of Matthew that strikes me: he holds on to his money as if to say, 'No, not me! No, this money is mine.' Here, this is me, a sinner on whom the Lord has turned his gaze. And this is what I said when they asked me if I would accept my election as pontiff." Then the pope whispers in Latin, "I am a sinner, but I trust in the infinite mercy and patience of our Lord Jesus Christ, and I accept in a spirit of penance."

Why Did You Become a Jesuit?

I UNDERSTAND THAT this motto of acceptance is for Pope Francis also a badge of identity. There was nothing left to add. I continue with the first question that I was going to ask: "Holy Father, what made you choose to enter the Society of Jesus? What struck you about the Jesuit order?"

"I wanted something more. But I did not know what. I entered the diocesan seminary. I liked the Dominicans, and I had Dominican friends. But then I chose the Society of Jesus, which I knew well because the seminary was entrusted to the Jesuits. Three things in particular struck me about the Society: the missionary spirit, community, and discipline. And this is strange, because I am a really, really undisciplined person. But their discipline, the way they manage their time—these things struck me so much.

"And then a thing that is really important for me: community. I was always looking for a community. I did not see myself as a priest on my own. I need a community. And you can tell this by the fact that I am here in Santa Marta. At the time of the conclave I lived in Room 207. (The rooms were assigned by drawing lots.) This room where we are now was a guest room. I chose to live here, in Room 201, because when I took possession of the papal apartment, inside myself I distinctly heard a 'no.' The papal apartment in the Apostolic Palace is not luxurious. It is old, tastefully decorated, and large, but not luxurious. But in the end it is like an inverted funnel. It is big and spacious, but the entrance is really tight. People can come only in dribs and drabs, and I cannot live without people. I need to live my life with others."

While the pope speaks about mission and community, I recall all of those documents of the Society of Jesus that talk about a "community for mission," and I find them among his words.

What Does It Mean for a Jesuit to Be Bishop of Rome?

I WANT TO continue along this line, and I ask the pope a question regarding the fact that he is the first Jesuit to be elected Bishop of Rome: "How do you understand the role of service to the universal church that you have been called to play in the light of Ignatian spirituality? What does it mean for a Jesuit to be elected pope? What element of Ignatian spirituality helps you live your ministry?"

"Discernment," he replies. "Discernment is one of the things that worked inside St. Ignatius. For him it is an instrument of struggle in order to know the Lord and follow him more closely. I was always struck by a saying that describes the vision of Ignatius: *Non coerceri a maximo, sed contineri a minimo divinum est* [Not to be limited by the greatest and yet to be contained in the tiniest—this is the divine]. I thought a lot about this phrase in connection with the issue of different roles in the government of the church, about becoming the superior of somebody else: it is important not to be restricted by a larger space, and it is important to be able to stay in restricted spaces. This virtue of the large and small is magnanimity. Thanks to magnanimity, we can always look at the horizon from the position where we are. That means being able to do the little things of every day with a big heart open to God and to others. That means being able to appreciate the small things inside large horizons, those of the kingdom of God.

"This motto," the pope continues, "offers parameters to assume a correct position for discernment, in order to hear the things of God from God's 'point of view.' According to St. Ignatius, great principles must be embodied in the circumstances of place, time, and people. In his own way, John XXIII adopted this attitude with regard to the government of the church, when he repeated the motto, 'See everything; turn a blind eye to much; correct a little.' John XXIII saw all things, the maximum dimension, but he chose to correct a few, the minimum dimension. You can have large projects and implement them by means of a few of the smallest things. Or you can use weak means that are more effective than strong ones, as Paul also said in his First Letter to the Corinthians.

"'This discernment takes time. For example, many think that changes and reforms can take place in a short time. I believe that we always need time to lay the foundations for real, effective change. And this is the time of discernment.

Sometimes discernment instead urges us to do precisely what you had at first thought you would do later. And that is what has happened to me in recent months. Discernment is always done in the presence of the Lord, looking at the signs, listening to the things that happen, the feeling of the people, especially the poor. My choices, including those related to the day-to-day aspects of life, like the use of a modest car, are related to a spiritual discernment that responds to a need that arises from looking at things, at people, and from reading the signs of the times. Discernment in the Lord guides me in my way of governing.

"But I am always wary of decisions made hastily. I am always wary of the first decision, that is, the first thing that comes to my mind if I have to make a decision. This is usually the wrong thing. I have to wait and assess, looking deep into myself, taking the necessary time. The wisdom of discernment redeems the necessary ambiguity of life and helps us find the most appropriate means, which do not always coincide with what looks great and strong."

The Society of Jesus

DISCERNMENT IS THEREFORE a pillar of the spirituality of Pope Francis. It expresses in a particular manner his Jesuit identity. I ask him then how the Society of Jesus can be of service to the church today, and what characteristics set it apart. I also ask him to comment on the possible risks that the Society runs.

"The Society of Jesus is an institution in tension," the pope replied, "always fundamentally in tension. A Jesuit is a person who is not centered in himself. The Society itself also looks to a center outside itself; its center is Christ and his church. So if the Society centers itself in Christ and the church, it has two fundamental points of reference for its balance and for being able to live on the margins, on the frontier. If it looks too much in upon itself, it puts itself at the center as a very solid, very well 'armed' structure, but then it runs the risk of feeling safe and self-sufficient. The Society must always have before itself the *Deus semper maior*, the always greater God, and the pursuit of the ever greater glory of God, the church as true bride of Christ our Lord, Christ the king who conquers us and to whom we offer our whole person and all our hard work, even if we are clay pots, inadequate. This tension takes us out of ourselves continuously. The tool that makes the Society of Jesus not centered in itself, really strong, is, then, the account of conscience, which is at the same time paternal and fraternal, because it helps the Society to fulfill its mission better."

The pope is referring to the requirement in the Constitutions of the Society of Jesus that the Jesuit must "manifest his conscience," that is, his inner spiritual situation, so that the superior can be more conscious and knowledgeable about sending a person on mission.

"But it is difficult to speak of the Society," continues Pope Francis. "When you express too much, you run the risk of being misunderstood. The Society of Jesus can be described only in narrative form. Only in narrative form do you discern, not in a philosophical or theological explanation, which allows you rather to discuss. The style of the Society is not shaped by discussion, but by discernment, which of course presupposes discussion as part of the process. The mystical dimension of discernment never defines its edges and does not complete the thought. The Jesuit must be a person whose thought is incomplete, in the sense of open-ended thinking. There have been periods in the

Society in which Jesuits have lived in an environment of closed and rigid thought, more instructive-ascetic than mystical: this distortion of Jesuit life gave birth to the *Epitome Instituti*."

The pope is referring to a compendium, first published in 1690 and reformulated in the twentieth century for practical purposes, that came to be seen as a replacement for the Constitutions. The formation of Jesuits for some time was shaped by this text, to the extent that some never read the Constitutions, the foundational text. During this period, in the pope's view, the rules threatened to overwhelm the spirit, and the Society yielded to the temptation to explicate and define its charism too narrowly.

Pope Francis continues: "No, the Jesuit always thinks, again and again, looking at the horizon toward which he must go, with Christ at the center. This is his real strength. And that pushes the Society to be searching, creative, and generous. So now, more than ever, the Society of Jesus must be contemplative in action, must live a profound closeness to the whole church as both the 'people of God' and 'holy mother the hierarchical church.' This requires much humility, sacrifice, and courage, especially when you are misunderstood or you are the subject of misunderstandings and slanders, but that is the most fruitful attitude. Let us think of the tensions of the past history, in the previous centuries, about the Chinese rites controversy, the Malabar rites, and the Reductions in Paraguay.

"I am a witness myself to the misunderstandings and problems that the Society has recently experienced. Among those there were tough times, especially when it came to the issue of extending to all Jesuits the fourth vow of obedience to the pope. What gave me confidence at the time of Father [Pedro] Arrupe [superior general of the Jesuits from 1965 to 1983] was the fact that he was a man of prayer, a man who spent much time in prayer. I remember him when he prayed sitting on the ground in the Japanese style. For this he had the right attitude and made the right decisions."

The Model: Peter Faber, "Reformed Priest"

I AM WONDERING if there are figures among the Jesuits, from the origins of the Society to the present date, that have affected him in a particular way, so I ask the pope who they are and why. He begins by mentioning Ignatius Loyola (founder of the Jesuits) and Francis Xavier, but then focuses on a figure that other Jesuits certainly know, but who is of course not as well known to the general public: Peter Faber [also known as Pierre Favre, 1506–46] from Savoy. He was one of the first companions of St. Ignatius—in fact the first—with whom he shared a room when the two were students at the University of Paris. The third roommate was Francis Xavier. Pius IX declared Faber blessed on September 5, 1872, and the cause for his canonization is still open.

The pope cites an edition of Faber's works, which he asked two Jesuit scholars, Miguel A. Fiorito and Jaime H. Amadeo, to edit and publish when he was provincial superior of the Jesuits in Argentina. An edition that he particularly likes is the one by Michel de Certeau. I ask the pope why he is so impressed by Faber and which of Faber's traits he finds particularly moving.

"[His] dialogue with all," the pope says, "even the most remote, and even with his opponents; his simple piety, a certain naïveté perhaps, his being available straightaway, his careful interior discernment, the fact that he was a man capable of great and strong decisions but also capable of being so gentle and loving."

As Pope Francis lists these personal characteristics of his favorite Jesuit, I understand just how much this figure has truly been a model for his own life. Michel de Certeau, SJ, characterized Faber simply as the "reformed priest," for whom interior experience, dogmatic expression, and structural reform are intimately inseparable. I begin to understand, therefore, that Pope Francis is inspired precisely by this kind of reform. At this point the pope continues with a reflection on the true face of the *fundador* of the Society of Jesus, Ignatius of Loyola.

"Ignatius is a mystic, not an ascetic," he says. "It irritates me when I hear that the Spiritual Exercises are 'Ignatian' only because they are done in silence. In fact, the Exercises can be perfectly Ignatian also in daily life and without the silence. An interpretation of the Spiritual Exercises that emphasizes asceticism, silence, and penance is a distorted one that became widespread even in the Society, especially in the Society of Jesus in Spain. I am rather close to the mystical movement, that of Louis Lallement and Jean-Joseph Surin. And Faber was a mystic."

Experience in Church Government

WHAT KIND OF experience in church government, as a Jesuit superior and then as superior of a province of the Society of Jesus, helped to fully form Father Bergoglio? The style of governance of the Society of Jesus involves decisions made by the superior, but also extensive consultation with his official advisers. So I ask, "Do you think that your past government experience can serve you in governing the universal church?"

After a brief pause for reflection, Pope Francis becomes very serious, but also very serene, and he responds: "In my experience as superior in the Society, to be honest, I have not always behaved in that way—that is, I did not always do the necessary consultation. And this was not a good thing. My style of government as a Jesuit at the beginning had many faults. That was a difficult time for the Society: an entire generation of Jesuits had disappeared. Because of this I found myself provincial when I was still very young. I was only thirty-six years old. That was crazy. I had to deal with difficult situations, and I made my decisions abruptly and by myself. Yes, but I must add one thing: When I entrust something to someone, I totally trust that person. He or she must make a really big mistake before I rebuke that person. But despite this, eventually people get tired of authoritarianism.

"My authoritarian and quick manner of making decisions led me to have serious problems and to be accused of being ultraconservative. I lived a time of great interior crisis when I was in Cordova. To be sure, I have never been like Blessed Imelda [a goody-goody], but I have never been a right-winger. It was my authoritarian way of making decisions that created problems.

"I say these things from life experience and because I want to make clear what the dangers are. Over time I learned many things. The Lord has allowed this growth in knowledge of government through my faults and my sins. So as Archbishop of Buenos Aires, I had a meeting with the six auxiliary bishops every two weeks, and several times a year with the council of priests. They asked questions, and we opened the floor for discussion. This greatly helped me to make the best decisions. But now I hear some people tell me: 'Do not consult too much, and decide by yourself.' Instead, I believe that consultation is very important.

"The consistories [of cardinals], the synods [of bishops] are, for example, important places to make real and active this consultation. We must, however, give them a less rigid form. I do not want token consultations, but real consultations. The consultation group of eight cardinals, this 'outsider' advisory group, is not only my decision, but it is the result of the will of the cardinals, as it was expressed in the general congregations before the conclave. And I want to see that this is a real, not ceremonial consultation."

Thinking with the Church

I KEEP MY questions focused on the theme of the church, and I ask Pope Francis what it means exactly for him to "think with the church," a notion St. Ignatius writes about in the *Spiritual Exercises*. He replies without hesitation and by using an image.

"The image of the church I like is that of the holy, faithful people of God. This is the definition I often use, and then there is that image from the Second Vatican Council's Dogmatic Constitution on the Church (No. 12). Belonging to a people has a strong theological value. In the history of salvation, God has saved a people. There is no full identity without belonging to a people. No one is saved alone, as an isolated individual, but God attracts us looking at the complex web of relationships that take place in the human community. God enters into this dynamic, this participation in the web of human relationships.

"The people itself constitutes a subject. And the church is the people of God on the journey through history, with joys and sorrows. Thinking with the church, therefore, is my way of being a part of this people. And all the faithful, considered as a whole, are infallible in matters of belief, and the people display this *infallibilitas in credendo,* this infallibility in believing, through a supernatural sense of the faith of all the people walking together. This is what I understand today as the 'thinking with the church' of which St. Ignatius speaks. When the dialogue among the people and the bishops and the pope goes down this road and is genuine, then it is assisted by the Holy Spirit. So this thinking with the church does not concern theologians only.

"This is how it is with Mary: if you want to know who she is, you ask theologians; if you want to know how to love her, you have to ask the people. In turn, Mary loved Jesus with the heart of the people, as we read in the Magnificat. We should not even think, therefore, that 'thinking with the church' means only thinking with the hierarchy of the church."

After a brief pause, Pope Francis emphasizes in a very direct manner the following point, in order to avoid misunderstandings: "And, of course, we must be very careful not to think that this *infallibilitas* of all the faithful I am talking about in the light of Vatican II is a form of populism. No, it is the experience of 'holy mother the hierarchical church,' as St. Ignatius called it, the church as the people of God, pastors and people together. The church is the totality of God's people.

"I see the sanctity of God's people, this daily sanctity," the pope continues. "There is a 'holy middle class,' which we can all be part of, the holiness Malègue wrote about." The pope is referring to Joseph Malègue, a French writer (1876–1940), particularly to the unfinished trilogy, *Black Stones: The Middle Classes of Salvation*. Some French literary critics have called Malègue the "Catholic Proust."

"I see the holiness," the pope continues, "in the patience of the people of God: a woman who is raising children, a man who works to bring home the bread, the sick, the elderly priests who have so many wounds but have a smile on their faces because they served the Lord, the sisters who work hard and live a hidden sanctity. This is for me the common sanctity. I often associate sanctity with patience: not only patience as *hypomenē* [the New Testament Greek word], taking charge of the events and circumstances of life, but also as a constancy in going forward, day by day. This is the sanctity of the militant church also mentioned by St. Ignatius. This was the sanctity of my parents: my dad, my mom, my grandmother Rosa, who loved me so much. In my breviary I have the last will of my grandmother Rosa, and I read it often. For me it is like a prayer. She is a saint who has suffered so much, also spiritually, and yet always went forward with courage.

"This church with which we should be thinking is the home of all, not a small chapel that can hold only a small group of selected people. We must not reduce the bosom of the universal church to a nest protecting our mediocrity. And the church is Mother; the church is fruitful. It must be. You see, when I perceive negative behavior in ministers of the church or in consecrated men or women, the first thing that comes to mind is: 'Here's an unfruitful bachelor' or 'Here's a spinster.' They are neither fathers nor mothers, in the sense that they have not been able to give spiritual life. Instead, for example, when I read the life of the Salesian missionaries who went to Patagonia, I read a story of the fullness of life, of fruitfulness.

"Another example from recent days that I saw got the attention of newspapers: the phone call I made to a young man who wrote me a letter. I called him because that letter was so beautiful, so simple. For me this was an act of generativity. I realized that he was a young man who is growing, that he saw in me a father, and that the letter tells something of his life to that father. The father cannot say, 'I do not care.' This type of fruitfulness is so good for me."

Young Churches and Ancient Churches

REMAINING WITH THE subject of the church, I ask the pope a question in light of the recent World Youth Day. This great event has turned the spotlight on young people, but also on those "spiritual lungs" that are the Catholic churches founded in historically recent times. "What," I ask, "are your hopes for the universal church that come from these churches?"

The pope replies: "The young Catholic churches, as they grow, develop a synthesis of faith, culture, and life, and so it is a synthesis different from the one developed by the ancient churches. For me, the relationship between the ancient Catholic churches and the young ones is similar to the relationship between young and elderly people in a society. They build the future, the young ones with their strength and the others with their wisdom. You always run some risks, of course. The younger churches are likely to feel self-sufficient; the ancient ones are likely to want to impose on the younger churches their cultural models. But we build the future together."

The Church as Field Hospital

POPE BENEDICT XVI, in announcing his resignation, said that the contemporary world is subject to rapid change and is grappling with issues of great importance for the life of faith. Dealing with these issues requires strength of body and soul, Pope Benedict said. I ask Pope Francis, in light of what he has just told me: "What does the church need most at this historic moment? Do we need reforms? What are your wishes for the church in the coming years? What kind of church do you dream of?"

Pope Francis, picking up on the introduction of my question, begins by showing great affection and immense respect for his predecessor. "Pope Benedict has done an act of holiness, greatness, humility. He is a man of God."

"I see clearly," the pope continues, "that the thing the church needs most today is the ability to heal wounds and to warm the hearts of the faithful; it needs nearness, proximity. I see the church as a field hospital after battle. It is useless to ask a seriously injured person if he has high cholesterol and about the level of his blood sugars! You have to heal his wounds. Then we can talk about everything else. Heal the wounds, heal the wounds. . . . And you have to start from the ground up.

"The church sometimes has locked itself up in small things, in small-minded rules. The most important thing is the first proclamation: Jesus Christ has saved you. And the ministers of the church must be ministers of mercy above all. The confessor, for example, is always in danger of being either too much of a rigorist or too lax. Neither is merciful, because neither of them really takes responsibility for the person. The rigorist washes his hands so that he leaves it to the commandment. The loose minister washes his hands by simply saying, 'This is not a sin' or something like that. In pastoral ministry we must accompany people, and we must heal their wounds.

"How are we treating the people of God? I dream of a church that is a mother and shepherdess. The church's ministers must be merciful, take responsibility for the people, and accompany them like the good Samaritan, who washes, cleans, and raises up his neighbor. This is pure gospel. God is greater than sin. The structural and organizational reforms are secondary—that is, they come afterward. The first reform must be the attitude. The ministers of the gospel must be people who can warm the hearts of the people, who walk through the dark night with them, who know how to dialogue and to descend themselves into their people's night, into the darkness, but without getting lost. The people of God want pastors, not clergy acting like bureaucrats or government officials. The bishops, particularly, must be able to support the movements of God among their people with patience, so that no one is left behind. But they must also be able to accompany the flock that has a flair for finding new paths.

"Instead of being just a church that welcomes and receives by keeping the doors open, let us try also to be a church that finds new roads, that is able to step outside itself and go to those who do not attend Mass, to those who have quit or are indifferent. The ones who quit sometimes do it for reasons that, if properly understood and assessed, can lead to a return. But that takes audacity and courage."

I take in what the pope is saying, and I mention that there are Christians who live in situations that from the point of view of the church are irregular or somewhat complex, Christians who, in one way or another, live with open wounds. I mention the divorced and remarried, same-sex couples, and other difficult situations. What kind of pastoral work can we do in these cases? What kinds of tools can we use?

The pope signals that he understands what I mean, and he responds. "We need to proclaim the gospel on every street corner," the pope says, "preaching the good news of the kingdom and healing, even with our preaching, every kind of disease and wound. In Buenos Aires I used to receive letters from homosexual persons who are 'socially wounded,' because they tell me that they feel like the church has always condemned them. But the church does not want to do this. During the return flight from Rio de Janeiro I said that if a homosexual person is of goodwill and is in search of God, I am no one to judge. By saying this, I said what the catechism says. Religion has the right to express its opinion in the service of the people, but God in creation has set us free: it is not possible to interfere spiritually in the life of a person.

"A person once asked me, in a provocative manner, if I approved of homosexuality. I replied with another question: 'Tell me, when God looks at a gay person, does he endorse the existence of this person with love, or reject and condemn this person?' We must always consider the person. Here we enter into the mystery of the human being. In life, God accompanies persons, and we must accompany them, starting from their situation. It is necessary to accompany them with mercy. When that happens, the Holy Spirit inspires the priest to say the right thing.

"This is also the great benefit of confession as a sacrament: evaluating case by case and discerning what is the best thing to do for a person who seeks God and grace. The confessional is not a torture chamber, but the place in which the Lord's mercy motivates us to do better. I also consider the situation of a woman with a failed marriage in her past and who also had an abortion. Then this woman remarries, and she is now happy and has five children. That abortion in her past weighs heavily on her conscience, and she sincerely regrets it. She would like to move forward in her Christian life. What is the confessor to do?

"We cannot insist only on issues related to abortion, gay marriage, and the use of contraceptive methods. This is not possible. I have not spoken much about these things, and I was reprimanded for that. But when we speak about these issues, we have to talk about them in a context. The teaching of the church, for that matter, is clear, and I am a son of the church, but it is not necessary to talk about these issues all the time.

"The dogmatic and moral teachings of the church are not all equivalent. The church's pastoral ministry cannot be obsessed with the transmission of a disjointed multitude of doctrines to be imposed insistently. Proclamation in a missionary style focuses on the essentials, on the necessary things: this is also what fascinates and attracts more, what makes the heart burn, as it did for the disciples at Emmaus. We have to find a new balance; otherwise even the moral edifice of the church is likely to fall like a house of cards, losing the freshness and fragrance of the gospel. The proposal of the gospel must be more simple, profound, radiant. It is from this proposition that the moral consequences then flow.

"I say this also thinking about the preaching and content of our preaching. A beautiful homily, a genuine sermon must begin with the first proclamation, with the proclamation of salvation. There is nothing more solid, deep, and sure than this proclamation. Then you have to do catechesis. Then you can draw even a moral consequence. But the proclamation of the saving love of God comes before moral and religious imperatives. Today sometimes it seems that the opposite order is prevailing. The homily is the touchstone to measure the pastor's proximity and ability to meet his people, because those who preach must recognize the heart of their community and must be able to see where the desire for God is lively and ardent. The message of the gospel, therefore, is not to be reduced to some aspects that, although relevant, on their own do not show the heart of the message of Jesus Christ."

A Religious Order Pope

POPE FRANCIS IS the first pontiff from a religious order since the Camaldolese monk Gregory XVI, who was elected in 1831. Thus I ask, "What is the specific place of religious men and women in the church of today?"

"Religious men and women are prophets," says the pope. "They are those who have chosen a following of Jesus that imitates his life in obedience to the Father, poverty, community life, and chastity. In this sense, the vows cannot end up being caricatures; otherwise, for example, community life becomes hell, and chastity becomes a way of life for unfruitful bachelors. The vow of chastity must be a vow of fruitfulness. In the church, the religious are called to be prophets in particular by demonstrating how Jesus lived on this earth, and to proclaim how the kingdom of God will be in its perfection.

"A religious must never give up prophecy. This does not mean opposing the hierarchical part of the church, although the prophetic function and the hierarchical structure do not coincide. I am talking about a proposal that is always positive, but it should not cause timidity. Let us think about what so many great saints, monks, and religious men and women have done, from St. Anthony the Abbot onward. Being prophets may sometimes imply making waves. I do not know how to put it. . . . Prophecy makes noise, uproar, some say 'a mess.' But in reality, the charism of religious people is like yeast: prophecy announces the spirit of the gospel."

The Roman Curia, Collegiality, and Ecumenism

FOLLOWING UP ON his reference to the hierarchy, at this point I ask the pope, "What do you think about the Roman dicasteries [the various departments that assist the pope in his mission]?"

"The dicasteries of the Roman Curia are at the service of the pope and the bishops," he says. "They must help both the particular churches and the bishops' conferences. They are instruments of help. In some cases, however, when they are not functioning well, they run the risk of becoming institutions of censorship. It is amazing to see the denunciations for lack of orthodoxy that come to Rome. I think the cases should be investigated by the local bishops' conferences, which can get valuable assistance from Rome. These cases, in fact, are much better dealt with locally. The Roman congregations are mediators; they are not middlemen or managers."

On June 29, during the ceremony of the blessing and imposition of the pallium on thirty-four metropolitan archbishops, Pope Francis spoke about "the path of collegiality" as the road that can lead the church to "grow in harmony with the service of primacy." So I ask, "How can we reconcile in harmony Petrine primacy and collegiality? Which roads are feasible also from an ecumenical perspective?"

The pope responds, "We must walk together: the people, the bishops, and the pope. Synodality should be lived at various levels. Maybe it is time to change the methods of the Synod of Bishops, because it seems to me that the current method is not dynamic. This will also have ecumenical value, especially with our Orthodox brethren. From them we can learn more about the meaning of episcopal collegiality and the tradition of synodality. The joint effort of reflection, looking at how the church was governed in the early centuries, before the breakup between East and West, will bear fruit in due time. In ecumenical relations it is important not only to know each other better, but also to recognize what the Spirit has sown in the other as a gift for us. I want to continue the discussion that was begun in 2007 by the joint [Catholic–Orthodox] commission on how to exercise the Petrine primacy, which led to the signing of the Ravenna Document. We must continue on this path."

I ask how Pope Francis envisions the future unity of the church in light of this response.

He answers, "We must walk united with our differences: there is no other way to become one. This is the way of Jesus."

Women in the Life of the Church

AND WHAT ABOUT the role of women in the church? The pope has made reference to this issue on several occasions. In an interview he had affirmed that the feminine presence in the church has not been able to sufficiently emerge: the temptation of male chauvinism has not left room to give visibility to the role that women deserve in the community. He took up this question again during his return trip from Rio de Janeiro, asserting that a profound theology of women has not yet been elaborated. So, I ask, "What should be the role of women in the church? What can be done to make their role more visible today?"

He answers: "It is necessary to broaden the opportunities for a stronger presence of women in the church. I am wary of a solution that can be reduced to a kind of 'female *machismo*,' because a woman has a different makeup than a man. But what I hear about the role of women is often inspired by an ideology of *machismo*. Women are asking deep questions that must be addressed. The church cannot be herself without the woman and her role. The woman is essential for the church. Mary, a woman, is more important than the bishops. I say this because we must not confuse the function with the dignity. We must therefore investigate further the role of women in the church. We have to work harder to develop a profound theology of the woman. Only by making this step will it be possible to better reflect on their function within the church. The feminine genius is needed wherever we make important decisions. The challenge today is this: to think about the specific place of women also in those places where the authority of the church is exercised for various areas of the church."

The Second Vatican Council

"WHAT DID THE Second Vatican Council accomplish?" I ask. "What does it mean?" In light of his previous affirmations, I imagine that he will deliver a long and articulate response. Instead, I get the impression that the pope simply considers the council an event that is not up for debate and that, as if to stress its fundamental importance, is not worth discussing at too great a length.

"Vatican II was a rereading of the Gospels in light of contemporary culture," says the pope. "Vatican II produced a renewal movement that simply comes from the same gospel. Its fruits are enormous. Just recall the liturgy. The work of liturgical reform has been a service to the people as a rereading of the Gospels from a concrete historical situation. Yes, there are hermeneutics of continuity and discontinuity, but one thing is clear: the dynamic of reading the Gospels, actualizing its message for today—which was typical of Vatican II—is absolutely irreversible. Then there are particular issues, like the liturgy according to the *Vetus Ordo* [the old ritual for the Mass]. I think the decision of Pope Benedict [his decision, of July 7, 2007, to allow a wider use of the Tridentine Mass] was prudent and motivated by the desire to help people who have this sensitivity. What is worrying, though, is the risk of the ideologization of the *Vetus Ordo*, its exploitation."

To Seek and Find God in All Things

POPE FRANCIS'S WORDS weigh heavily upon addressing the challenges of today. Years ago he had written that, in order to see reality, one must look with a gaze of faith. Otherwise one sees only small pieces of a fragmented reality. This is also one of the themes of the encyclical *Lumen Fidei*. I am also thinking of a few passages from Pope Francis's speeches during the World Youth Day in Rio de Janeiro. I quote them to him: "God is real if he shows himself in the here and now." "God is everywhere." These are phrases that echo the Ignatian expression "to seek and find God in all things." Therefore I ask, "Your Holiness, how does one seek and find God in all things?"

"What I said in Rio referred to the time in which we seek God," he answers. "In fact, there is a temptation to seek God in the past or in a possible future. God is certainly in the past because we can see the footprints. And God is also in the future as a promise. But the 'concrete' God, so to speak, is today. For this reason, complaining never helps us find God. The complaints of today about how 'barbaric' the world is—these complaints sometimes end up giving birth within the church to desires to establish order in the sense of pure conservation, as a defense. No, God is to be encountered in the world of today.

"God manifests himself in historical revelation, in history. Time initiates processes, and space crystallizes them. God is in history, in the processes.

"We must not focus on occupying the spaces where power is exercised, but rather on starting long-run historical processes. We must initiate processes rather than occupy spaces. God manifests himself in time and is present in the processes of history. This gives priority to actions that give birth to new historical dynamics. And it requires patience, waiting.

"Finding God in all things is not an empirical 'Eureka!' When we desire to encounter God, we would like to verify him immediately by an empirical method. But you cannot meet God this way. God is found in the gentle breeze perceived by Elijah. The senses that find God are the ones St. Ignatius called spiritual senses. Ignatius asks us to open our spiritual sensitivity to encounter God beyond a purely empirical approach. A contemplative attitude is necessary: it is the feeling that you are moving along the good path of understanding and affection toward things and situations. Profound peace, spiritual consolation, love of God, and love of all things in God—this is the sign that you are on this right path."

Certitude and Mistakes

I ASK, "SO if the encounter with God is not an empirical 'Eureka!' and if it is a journey that sees with the eyes of history, then we can also make mistakes?"

The pope replies: "Yes, in this quest to seek and find God in all things there is still an area of uncertainty. There must be. If a person says that he met God with total certainty and is not touched by a margin of uncertainty, then this is not good. For me, this is an important key. If one has the answers to all the questions—that is the proof that God is not with him. It means that he is a false prophet using religion for himself. The great leaders of the people of God, like Moses, have always left room for doubt. You must leave room for the Lord, not for our certainties; we must be humble. Uncertainty is in every true discernment that is open to finding confirmation in spiritual consolation.

"The risk in seeking and finding God in all things, then, is the willingness to explain too much, to say with human certainty and arrogance, 'God is here.' We will find only a god that fits our measure. The correct attitude is that of St. Augustine: seek God to find him, and find God to keep searching for God forever. Often we seek as if we were blind, as one often reads in the Bible. And this is the experience of the great fathers of the faith, who are our models. We have to reread the Letter to the Hebrews, Chapter 11. Abraham leaves his home without knowing where he was going, by faith. All of our ancestors in the faith died seeing the good that was promised, but from a distance. . . . Our life is not given to us like an opera libretto, in which all is written down; but it means going, walking, doing, searching, seeing. . . . We must enter into the adventure of the quest for meeting God; we must let God search and encounter us.

"Because God is first; God is always first and makes the first move. God is a bit like the almond flower of your Sicily, Antonio, which always blooms first. We read it in the Prophets. God is encountered walking, along the path. At this juncture, someone might say that this is relativism. Is it relativism? Yes, if it is misunderstood as a kind of indistinct pantheism. It is not relativism if it is understood in the biblical sense, that God is always a surprise, so you never know where and how you will find him. You are not setting the time and place of the encounter with him. You must, therefore, discern the encounter. Discernment is essential.

"If the Christian is a restorationist, a legalist, if he wants everything clear and safe, then he will find nothing. Tradition and memory of the past must help us to have the courage to open up new areas to God. Those who today always look for disciplinarian solutions, those who long for an exaggerated doctrinal 'security,' those who stubbornly try to recover a past that no longer exists—they have a static and inward-directed view of things. In this way, faith becomes an ideology among other ideologies. I have a dogmatic certainty: God is in every person's life. God is in everyone's life. Even if the life of a person has been a disaster, even if it is destroyed by vices, drugs, or anything else— God is in this person's life. You can, you must try to seek God in every human life. Although the life of a person is a land full of thorns and weeds, there is always a space in which the good seed can grow. You have to trust God."

Must We Be Optimistic?

THE POPE'S WORDS remind me of some of his past reflections, in which as a cardinal he wrote that God is already living in the city, in the midst of all and united to each. It is another way, in my opinion, to say what St. Ignatius wrote in the *Spiritual Exercises,* that God "labors and works" in our world. So I ask, "Do we have to be optimistic? What are the signs of hope in today's world? How can I be optimistic in a world in crisis?"

"I do not like to use the word *optimism,* because that is about a psychological attitude," the pope says. "I like to use the word *hope* instead, according to what we read in the Letter to the Hebrews, Chapter 11, that I mentioned before. The fathers of the faith kept walking, facing difficulties. And hope does not disappoint, as we read in the Letter to the Romans. Think instead of the first riddle of Puccini's opera *Turandot,*" the pope suggests.

At that moment I recalled more or less by heart the verses of the riddle of the princess in that opera, to which the solution is hope:

In the gloomy night flies an iridescent ghost.
It rises and opens its wings
on the infinite black humanity.
The whole world invokes it
and the whole world implores it.
But the ghost disappears with the dawn
to be reborn in the heart.
And every night it is born
and every day it dies!

These are verses that reveal the desire for hope. Yet here that hope is an iridescent ghost that disappears with the dawn.

"See," says Pope Francis, "Christian hope is not a ghost, and it does not deceive. It is a theological virtue and therefore, ultimately, a gift from God that cannot be reduced to optimism, which is only human. God does not mislead hope; God cannot deny himself. God is all promise."

Art and Creativity

I AM STRUCK by the reference the pope just made to Puccini's *Turandot* while speaking of the mystery of hope. I would like to understand better his artistic and literary references. I remind him that in 2006 he said that great artists know how to present the tragic and painful realities of life with beauty. So I ask who are the artists and writers he prefers, and if they have something in common.

"I have really loved a diverse array of authors. I love very much Dostoevsky and Hölderlin. I remember Hölderlin for that poem written for the birthday of his grandmother that is very beautiful and was spiritually very enriching for me. The poem ends with the verse, 'May the man hold fast to what the child has promised.' I was also impressed because I loved my grandmother Rosa, and in that poem Hölderlin compares his grandmother to the Virgin Mary, who gave birth to Jesus, the friend of the earth who did not consider anybody a foreigner.

"I have read *The Betrothed*, by Alessandro Manzoni, three times, and I have it now on my

table, because I want to read it again. Manzoni
gave me so much. When I was a child, my grandmother taught me by heart the beginning of *The
Betrothed*: 'That branch of Lake Como that turns
off to the south between two unbroken chains of
mountains . . .' I also liked Gerard Manley Hop-
kins very much.

"Among the great painters, I admire Caravaggio;
his paintings speak to me. But also Chagall, with
his *White Crucifixion*. Among musicians I love Mozart, of course. The "Et Incarnatus Est" from his
Mass in C Minor is matchless; it lifts you to God! I
love Mozart performed by Clara Haskil. Mozart ful-
fills me. But I cannot think about his music; I have
to listen to it. I like listening to Beethoven, but in a
Promethean way, and the most Promethean inter-
preter for me is Furtwängler. And then Bach's *Pas-
sions*. The piece by Bach that I love so much is the
"Erbarme Dich," the tears of Peter in the *St. Matthew Passion*. Sublime. Then, at a different level,
not intimate in the same way, I love Wagner. I like
to listen to him, but not all the time. The perfor-
mance of Wagner's *Ring* by Furtwängler at La Scala
in Milan in 1950 is for me the best. But also the
Parsifal by Knappertsbusch in 1962.

"We should also talk about the cinema. *La
Strada*, by Fellini, is the movie that perhaps
I loved the most. I identify with this movie, in
which there is an implicit reference to St. Francis.

I also believe that I watched all of the Italian movies with Anna Magnani and Aldo Fabrizi when I was between ten and twelve years old. Another film that I loved is *Rome, Open City*. I owe my film culture especially to my parents, who used to take us to the movies quite often.

"Anyway, in general I love tragic artists, especially classical ones. There is a nice definition that Cervantes puts on the lips of the bachelor Carrasco to praise the story of Don Quixote: 'Children have it in their hands, young people read it, adults understand it, the elderly praise it.' For me this can be a good definition of the classics."

I realize that I have become utterly engrossed in these artistic references of his. I desire to enter into his life by passing through the door of his artistic choices. I imagine it would be a long journey, but certainly a journey worth taking. It would also include cinema, from Italian neorealism to *Babette's Feast*. Other authors and other works now come to my mind, authors and works that he has mentioned in other occasions, also minor, or less famous, or even local ones: from the epic poem *Martín Fierro* by José Hernández, to the poetry of Nino Costa, to *The Great Exodus* by Luigi Orsenigo. I also think of Joseph Malègue and José María Pemán. Clearly I think of famous writers like Dante and Borges, but also of the Argentine writer Leopoldo Marechal, the author of the novels *Adán Buenos-*

ayres, The Banquet of Severo Arcangelo, and *Megaphone, or War.*

I think especially about Borges, a writer with whom Father Bergoglio had direct contact in his earlier years. Back then he was a twenty-eight-year-old teacher of literature at the Colegio de la Inmaculada Concepción in Santa Fe, Argentina. Father Bergoglio taught students during their last two years of secondary school and encouraged his pupils to take up creative writing. When I was younger, I too had an experience just like his. Then, I taught at the Istituto Massimo of Rome, where I also founded the creative cultural project known as "BombaCarta." I tell him the story. Finally I ask the pope to tell me about his own experience with teaching.

"It was a bit risky," he answers. "I had to make sure that my students read *El Cid.* But the boys did not like it. They wanted to read García Lorca. Then I decided that they would study *El Cid* at home and that in class I would teach the authors the boys liked the most. Of course, young people wanted to read more 'racy' literary works, like the contemporary *La Casada Infiel* or classics like *La Celestina,* by Fernando de Rojas. But by reading these things they acquired a taste in literature, poetry, and we went on to other authors. And that was for me a great experience. I completed the program, but in an unstructured way—that is, not ordered according to what we expected in the beginning, but in an order that came naturally by reading these authors. And this mode befitted me: I did not like to have a rigid schedule, but rather I liked to know where we had to go with the readings, with a rough sense of where we were headed. Then I also started to get them to write. In the end I decided to send Borges two stories written by my boys. I knew his secretary, who had been my piano teacher. And Borges liked those stories very much. And then he set out to write the introduction to a collection of these writings."

"Then, Holy Father, creativity is important for the life of a person?" I ask.

He laughs and replies, "For a Jesuit it is extremely important! A Jesuit must be creative."

Frontiers and Laboratories

CREATIVITY, THEREFORE, is important for a Jesuit. Pope Francis, during a visit with the Jesuit priests and other staff members of *La Civiltà Cattolica,* had articulated a triad of important characteristics relevant to the cultural initiatives of the Jesuits. I turn my thoughts to that day, June 14, 2013. I recall that back then, in a conversation just before the meeting with the entire group, the pope had already informed me about this triad: dialogue, discernment, frontier. And he insisted particularly on the last point, quoting Pope Paul VI. In a well-known speech, Paul VI had spoken directly about the Jesuits: "Wherever in the church—even in the most difficult and extreme fields, in the crossroads of ideologies, in the social trenches—there has been and is now conversation between the deepest desires of human beings and the perennial message of the gospel, Jesuits have been and are there."

I ask Pope Francis for a further explanation: "You asked us to be careful not to fall into 'the temptation to tame the frontiers': one must go out to the frontiers, not bring the frontiers home in order to paint them a bit artificially and tame them. What were you referring to? What exactly did you wish to tell us? This interview, as you know, was organized by a group of magazines directed by the Society of Jesus. What invitation do you wish to extend to them? What should their priorities be?"

"The three key words that I commended to *La Civiltà Cattolica* can be extended to all the journals of the Society, perhaps with different emphases according to their natures and their objectives. When I insist on the frontier, I am referring in a particular way to the need for those who work in the world of culture to be inserted into the context in which they operate and on which they reflect. There is always the lurking danger of living in a laboratory. Ours is not a 'lab faith,' but a 'journey faith,' a historical faith. God has revealed himself as history, not as a compendium of abstract truths. I am afraid of laboratories, because in the laboratory you take the problems and then you bring them home to tame them, to paint them artificially, out of their context. You cannot bring home the frontier, but you have to live on the border and be audacious."

I ask for examples from his personal experience.

"When it comes to social issues, it is one thing to have a meeting to study the problem of drugs in a slum neighborhood and quite another thing to go there, live there, understand the problem from the inside, and study it. There is a brilliant letter by Father Arrupe to the Centers for Social Research and Action on poverty, in which he says clearly that one cannot speak of poverty if one does not experience poverty, with a direct connection to the places in which there is poverty. The word *insertion* is dangerous, because some religious have taken it as a fad, and disasters have occurred because of a lack of discernment. But it is truly important.

"The frontiers are many. Let us think of the religious sisters living in hospitals. They live on the frontier. I am alive because of one of them. When I went through my lung disease at the hospital, the doctor gave me penicillin and streptomycin in certain doses. The sister who was on duty tripled my doses because she was daringly astute; she knew what to do because she was with ill people all day. The doctor, who really was a good one, lived in his laboratory; the sister lived on the frontier and was in dialogue with it every day. Domesticating the frontier means just talking from a remote location, locking yourself up in a laboratory. Laboratories are useful, but reflection for us must always start from experience."

Human Self-Understanding

I ASK THE pope if and how this is also true in the case of another important cultural frontier, the anthropological challenge. The understanding of human existence to which the church has traditionally referred as well as the language in which the church has expressed it remain solid points of reference and are the result of centuries-long experience and wisdom. However, the human beings to whom the church is speaking no longer seem to understand these notions, nor do they consider them sufficient. I begin to advance the idea that we now interpret ourselves in a different way than in the past, using different categories. This is also due to the great changes in society as well as a broader conception of what it means to be human.

At this point the pope stands up and takes the breviary from his desk. It is in Latin and is worn down by continued use. He opens it to the Office of the Readings of the *Feria Sexta,* that is, Friday, of the 27th week. He reads a passage to me taken from the *Commonitorium Primum* of St. Vincent of Lerins: *"Ita etiam christianae religionis dogma sequatur has decet profectuum leges, ut annis sci-licet consolidetur, dilatetur tempore, sublimetur aetate* [Thus even the dogma of the Christian religion must proceed from these laws. It progresses, solidifying with years, growing over time, deepening with age]."

The pope comments: "St. Vincent of Lerins makes a comparison between the biological development of man and the transmission from one era to another of the deposit of faith, which grows and is strengthened with time. Here, human self-understanding changes with time, and so also human consciousness deepens. Let us think of when slavery was accepted or the death penalty was allowed without any problem. So we grow in the understanding of the truth. Exegetes and theologians help the church to mature in her own judgment. Even the other sciences and their development help the church in its growth in understanding. There are ecclesiastical rules and precepts that were once effective, but now they have lost value or meaning. The view of the church's teaching as a monolith to defend without nuance or different understandings is wrong.

"After all, in every age of history, humans try to understand and express themselves better. So human beings in time change the way they perceive themselves. It's one thing for a man who expresses himself by carving the Winged Victory of Samothrace, yet another for Caravaggio, Chagall, and yet another still for Dalí. Even the forms for expressing truth can be multiform, and this is indeed necessary for the transmission of the gospel in its timeless meaning.

"Humans are in search of themselves, and of course in this search they can also make mistakes. The church has experienced times of brilliance, like that of Thomas Aquinas. But the church has lived also times of decline in its ability to think. For example, we must not confuse the genius of Thomas Aquinas with the age of decadent Thomist commentaries. Unfortunately, I studied philosophy from textbooks that came from decadent or largely bankrupt Thomism. In thinking of the human being, therefore, the church should strive for genius and not for decadence.

"When does a formulation of thought cease to be valid? When it loses sight of the human or even when it is afraid of the human or deluded about itself. The deceived thought can be depicted as Ulysses encountering the song of the Siren, or as Tannhäuser in an orgy surrounded by satyrs and bacchantes, or as Parsifal, in the second act of Wagner's opera, in the palace of Klingsor. The thinking of the church must recover genius and better understand how human beings understand themselves today, in order to develop and deepen the church's teaching."

Prayer

I ASK POPE Francis about his preferred way to pray.

"I pray the breviary every morning. I like to pray with the psalms. Then, later, I celebrate Mass. I pray the Rosary. What I really prefer is adoration in the evening, even when I get distracted and think of other things, or even fall asleep praying. In the evening then, between seven and eight o'clock, I stay in front of the Blessed Sacrament for an hour in adoration. But I pray mentally even when I am waiting at the dentist or at other times of the day.

"Prayer for me is always a prayer full of memory, of recollection, even the memory of my own history or what the Lord has done in his church or in a particular parish. For me it is the memory of which St. Ignatius speaks in the First Week of the Exercises in the encounter with the merciful Christ crucified. And I ask myself: 'What have I done for Christ? What am I doing for Christ? What should I do for Christ?' It is the memory of which Ignatius speaks in the 'Contemplation for Experiencing Divine Love,' when he asks us to recall the gifts we have received. But above all, I also know that the Lord remembers me. I can forget about him, but I know that he never, ever forgets me. Memory has a fundamental role for the heart of a Jesuit: memory of grace, the memory mentioned in Deuteronomy, the memory of God's works that are the basis of the covenant between God and the people. It is this memory that makes me his son and that makes me a father too."

I realize that I could continue on with this conversation, but I know that, in the words of the pope himself, I ought not "mistreat the limits." All in all, we spoke together for more than six hours over the course of three meetings on August 19, 23, and 29, 2013. For the sake of continuity, I have chosen to write up our dialogue as one text, without marking the starting and stopping points of our various sessions. Our time together was, in truth, more a conversation than an interview, and my questions served simply to guide the discussion in a general sense, rather than enclose it within rigid and predefined parameters. From a linguistic point of view, we frequently shifted back and forth between Spanish and Italian, often without even noticing. There was nothing mechanical about it, and the answers were the result of an extended dialogue and a line of reasoning that I have tried to render here in a concise manner and to the best of my abilities.

Part Two

Responses

A New Way of Being Church

Pope Francis Encourages Us to Be Comfortable with Uncertainty

Timothy Radcliffe, OP

POPE FRANCIS BEGINS his interview with *America* with a reference to Caravaggio's *The Calling of St. Matthew,* an image that unlocks that which is at the heart of his life and mission. Jesus looks at Matthew, bent over his money. Francis identifies with the man: "Here, this is me, a sinner on whom the Lord has turned his gaze." But he also sees the Christian mission as offering that healing gaze to others. He is touched by seeing how individuals live. When he addresses the question of welcoming gay people in the church, he says, "Tell me, when God looks at a gay person, does he endorse the existence of this person with love, or reject and condemn this person?" If we dare to really see people, in their dignity and humanity, then we shall discover the right words to say. Who knows where this will take us?

The interview focuses on Francis's identity as the first Jesuit pope. As a Dominican, I am delighted that at last the Society has one. We Dominicans have had four, and since the time of Pope St. Pius V in the sixteenth century, the pope has even worn a form of Dominican habit! However, Pope Francis is influenced profoundly by the founders of two religious orders, Francis and Ignatius. It would have been interesting to explore the interplay of both traditions. If we are to escape narrowness, we always need several perspectives to edge us forward.

As a Jesuit, the pope gives a central place to discernment. This implies patience, taking the time to think, pray, and consult. This is vital for understanding what is happening in these early days of his pontificate. People are impatient to see what he will do, but he says, "I believe that we always need time to lay the foundations for real, effective change. . . . I am always wary of decisions made hastily." This contradicts the pressure of the media to wrap people up in simple categories. Uncertainty is unbearable. We have to feel our way forward: "The Jesuit always thinks, again and again, looking at the horizon toward which he must go, with Christ at the center."

Pope Francis says that "the structural and organizational reforms are secondary—that is, they come afterward. The first reform must be the attitude." Structural change to the government of the church is vital, but it must follow from a new way of *being* church, in which we get out of the sacristy, engage with people, know their suffering and their puzzlement from within. At this stage, the pope is showing the way forward by what he does. He has a capacity to make expansive gestures that open up new perspectives. His first trip outside Rome was a visit to Lampedusa, where so many immigrants have died trying to enter Europe; or think of his visit to the *favela* in Rio de Janeiro. Christianity is a religion of sacramental gestures, the pouring of water and the breaking of bread, and his gestures are powerful in opening up the future.

This new way of being church will eventually have to find structural form. Pope Francis says, "The dicasteries of the Roman Curia are at the service of the pope and the bishops." It has not always felt this way! Cardinal Basil Hume, the late archbishop of Westminster, said that the bishops must cease to be at the service of the pope and the Roman Curia, but rather the Curia serve the government of the pope and the bishops. This implies that the pope ceases to be a monarch, presiding over the church from a remote height, and becomes again the bishop of Rome, embedded in the college of bishops. From the moment that he stepped onto the balcony of St. Peter's, Francis has shown that this is his intention. So this papacy could mark the most fundamental change in the governance of the church in centuries, from monarchy to collegiality. Much of Pope Emeritus Benedict's theology of the church implied shift. Francis wishes to *do* it. He insists on the return to models of synodal government and on real consultation. Laypeople will have a voice, as they often did in the early church. We must have patience as the form of this new structure and dynamic unfolds.

I would conclude with two profound hopes: that a way will be found to welcome divorced and remarried people back to communion and, most important, that women will be given real authority and voice in the church. The pope expresses his desire that this may happen, but what concrete form can it take? He believes that the ordination of women to the ministerial priesthood is not possible, but decision making in the church has become ever more closely linked to ordination in recent years. Can that bond be loosened? Let us hope that women may be ordained to the diaconate and so have a place in preaching at the Eucharist. What other ways can authority be shared?

Timothy Radcliffe, OP, *is former master general of the Dominican order and the author of* What Is the Point of Being a Christian?

A Pope Engaged with the World

Francis Hears the Cries of His Flock

Karen Sue Smith

AFTER READING NEWS reports about the interview with Pope Francis, I read the full text. What struck me initially were the breadth and depth of the pope's remarks in addressing the sweeping questions the editors put to him. Instead of centering on the church's "obsession," as the pope put it, with contraception, abortion, and same sex marriage, the text ranges widely. It reveals the pope's joyful engagement with this world, its people and culture. "God is in every person's life," Pope Francis declares, with no exceptions. And God is in our own history.

In reading the entire interview, one glimpses the pope as an inquisitive child, as a young man called to the priesthood, as a priest with so much potential that he was promoted to leadership too early and made some mistakes in governance. His authoritarian style, he admits, made him seem right-wing. From his mistakes, however, he has learned to listen, to value collaboration, and to practice discernment. The pope reveals himself as a complex person. He is a holy man of prayer, an empathetic pastor, a discerning Jesuit, a family man deeply influenced by his grandmother, and a loving father who as *il papa* eagerly cares for his "children" in the church. He is also the director of a field hospital whose mission is to heal the world's wounded with the gospel. Though troubled by war, poverty, and injustice, he remains full of mercy and hope.

That said, it seems to me that the media's convergence on a single point from this long interview as "the news"—namely, the pope's desire to change (or at least put on hold) the church's obsession with moral condemnations of sex-related sins—confirms the pope's insight that the church's priorities urgently need fixing. Pope Francis gets it. He understands what is vital: how others see the church and why that matters; what the contemporary world needs from the church; how the people of God together ensure the faith (infallibly, he says); what synods and local bishops' conferences could contribute, if empowered; and how the Curia should help church leaders rather than run the church. Hooray!

Even if only a few of these insights were to be actualized, the church would be improved immensely. Some doors and windows might be opened again, a welcome mat rolled out. If it is not too late, young people might even give the church a look. (Watch out for the spin and backlash, though, as others seek to reinterpret the pope's words for their own purposes. It has already begun.)

What strikes me as most lasting is the pope's personal example. Like Francis, the beloved saint, Pope Francis seems truly to love the people of this world. He embodies the compassion of Jesus, which attracts followers, not just fans, and changes lives. This pope wants to walk with us, says he needs us to be his "community." And this same pope who relishes great art, books, films, and music has an ear attuned to the cry of the poor and wants to serve them. History will remember that.

Karen Sue Smith *is former editorial director of* America.

Francis the Witness

The Pope Presents a Fresh Vision of the Gospel

Bishop Blase J. Cupich

REPORTERS AND COMMENTATORS, both secular and religious, are reading the tea leaves, trying to find hidden meanings and clues by parsing and analyzing the pope's interview published in Jesuit periodicals. What did he say, and what did he not say? Do his words signal major changes in policy and practice for Catholics?

David Brooks feels this approach is a distraction from the real power of the interview. In his comments on the interview with Pope Francis during the PBS *NewsHour* on September 20, he said, "What we should focus on is the personality of Francis, a remarkable personality . . . a gorgeous personality of humility, of spirituality, of religiosity. If you just read that interview, you see a man you tremendously admire, who I think is going to have a tremendous effect on the world." In other words, Francis shows himself as a witness more than a teacher. He is teaching because he is a witness, and being a witness, he reveals himself. This should be our focus, Brooks suggests. No interpretation, no parsing is needed. Instead of reading the tea leaves, we should drink the tea.

Pope Francis tells us who he is by pointing to Caravaggio's *The Calling of St. Matthew*: "Here, this is me, a sinner on whom the Lord has turned his gaze." He is telling us that he has experienced the same rush of speechless wonder and graced love Caravaggio depicts in his painting. In a darkened corner flooded by a sudden ray of light, the tax collector sits in stunned disbelief that he is being singled out for discipleship. This is Jorge Mario Bergoglio's story. The impact of seeing the face of God anew, a face that radiates first and foremost with graced compassion, has changed his life. But, even more, it has left him with an unquenchable thirst "to know the Lord and follow Him more closely."

As a result, all other attachments are relative, and he is centered in pursuing more and more the One who mercifully loves him, seeking God, discerning God's activity and will in all things. This is why he is patient, not impulsive, in making decisions; why he is attentive "to the things that happen, the feeling of the people, especially the poor"; and why thinking with the church means being part of "the people of God on the journey through history, with joys and sorrows."

The point is simple. His words cannot be understood apart from his witness. In this interview, content and form converge. Analyzing it for hints of particular changes in ecclesial policy and practice may be more entertaining, but, like entertainment, it is a diversion. We should focus on a person who reveals himself as a fresh witness of the gospel, who is stirring our hearts to take up the journey with him as a fellow disciple with new vigor and purpose. His words and witness are an invitation to humbly and actively seek God working in the world and in the people called to be God's own.

Each of us needs to take the time to reflect on how to respond to this "extemporaneous encyclical," as the commentator Michael Gerson calls it. But, even now, as a diocesan bishop for fifteen years, I can already identify some areas of my ministry of teaching, sanctifying, and governing that will benefit. These initially come to mind:

1. Catechesis, preaching, and passing on the faith must not only be about educating the members of our communities in the content of our tradition. This is important, but it must equally be about developing their spiritual sensitivity to the ways God manifests His presence and action in

the world. Schooling people in the ways of on-going discernment produces a greater receptivity to the tradition of the church and at the same time creates the freedom that will make them more responsive to the will of God throughout their lives. This balance is in keeping with the Lord's great commission: "Go teach *and* make disciples."

2. Pope Francis's emphasis on the ongoing discernment of the action and will of the ever merciful One also has implications for our worship and the promotion of communion among Christians. As the source and summit of Christian life, the liturgy needs to be the celebration that reveals His saving and redeeming work taking place through and in the midst of the people called to be His own. Reflecting that aspiration more fully in our multicultural communities makes the task of inculturation all the more urgent.

3. Similarly, instead of a minimalist approach to promoting ecumenism by healing differences and reconciling the past, the work of Christian unity becomes foremost an opportunity to look for how God is working in our separated brothers and sisters and to "recognize what the Spirit has sown in the other as a gift for us," as Francis says.

4. Collaborative governance needs to be more than calling on the advice and competence of others to make up for our episcopal shortcomings. Rather, governance involves seeking how God is revealing his work through others in the community. Rather than limiting our consultation to those with financial and legal abilities, we also need to listen to those who work side by side with the poor each day and who are on the front lines in health care, education, and other fields of ministry. We diminish our effectiveness when we do not call on these brothers and sisters to gain insight before making decisions in these areas. But, even more important, we pass up the chance to see how God is working through them and to more fully know God's will.

Francis offers the witness of one who has personally internalized and who himself lives what he preaches and proclaims. This is the essential feature of true evangelization, which Paul VI had in mind in *Evangelii Nuntiandi* (1975): "Modern man listens more willingly to witnesses than to teachers, and if he does listen to teachers, it is because they are witnesses." Ultimately it is only the witness who convinces people, not the teacher.

This is why Brooks calls him a gorgeous personality and, like others, admires Francis, the humble witness, as one who "is going to have a tremendous effect on the world." The effect is already being felt. It is time to put away the tea leaves and drink the tea.

Most Rev. Blase J. Cupich *is bishop of Spokane.*

Alleluia!

Cardinal Timothy M. Dolan

KEVIN CLARKE, SENIOR editor at *America*, asked New York's Cardinal Timothy M. Dolan for his reaction to the interview with Pope Francis published in *America*. Here is what he had to say:

AMERICA: Many found Pope Francis's words blunt and more than a little shocking. What was your gut reaction?

DOLAN: My gut reaction? "Yippie!" I wanted to sing out loud, "Alleluia!" For one, I was so exhilarated that a pope would even sit down for such a lengthy personal interview. All of us take risks in doing this—as I am right now with you—but it's worth the risk. Then, to have a pope get so personal about his style of prayer, his models of holiness, his hopes and frustrations. It reminded me of an ancient title for the Bishop of Rome, Servant of the Servants of God. He's not aloof from us, above us. To use his words, he's walking with us.

AMERICA: How do you think U.S. bishops will respond?

DOLAN: The jury's back. We bishops welcome and applaud his remarks. We bishops have placed the "new evangelization" as our top priority, as both Blessed John Paul II and Pope Emeritus Benedict asked us. We realize that perception is a pivotal factor in the effectiveness of that sacred task. If the church is perceived as crabby, nagging, hung up on a few "pet peeves," or judgmental, as unjust and inaccurate as that perception might be, we can't evangelize very well. What Pope Francis has done is popped the blister of that perception, and we bishops cheer him on. We are about a yes, not about a no.

AMERICA: Some, who have felt marginalized by the church, have found great hope in the pope's remarks. Others, who prefer perhaps a more disciplined, doctrinally oriented church, have apparently been thrown for a loop by them. Are both sides missing something or is it possible that his positions could lead to even more discord within the church, rather than the healing Pope Francis seems to be seeking?

DOLAN: Yeah, both sides miss something, or rather someone. Pope Francis is probably frustrated that all the attention is on him, his interview, his statements. He wants the attention on Jesus. What he's really telling us is, first things first! Seek ye first . . . ! If we emphasize Jesus, his person, teaching, salvation, invitation, death, and resurrection, everything else works out. My friend Father Bob Barron observes that, when he helps a foreign visitor who wants to understand baseball, he doesn't start with a technicality like the infield fly rule. Start with the beauty, majesty, poetry, legend of the drama of the game! That's what the Holy Father is suggesting: Start with Jesus, the way, the truth, the life. Start with the truth, not the consequences!

AMERICA: You have certainly been considered a welcoming face of the church in your day-to-day ministry, but based on the pope's comments, are you reconsidering any aspect of your strategy, if that's the right word, of engagement with American culture, secularists, lapsed Catholics, regular pew sitters?

DOLAN: Thanks. I hope so. I'm a rookie compared to Francis. Yes, his observations on discernment move me. I'm always worried about where God seems to be absent. But Francis reminds me He's always there, I'm just not noticing Him. That takes discernment. Where is He as I decide to merge a parish? Where is He as I mull over the budget? Where is He as I worry about dwindling Mass attendance? Pope Francis claims He's there! In all those neuralgic areas where we think He's sleeping . . . No. He's there. I better discern that presence and that direction.

The Call of the Spirit

The Style and Substance of Pope Francis

James Hanvey, SJ

WE THINK WE know the papacy and tend not to expect many surprises from the Vatican. Indeed, part of its "mystique" lies in its apparent immunity to historical change. Yet it does change, and it does surprise us. Whether it was the unexpected decision of John XXIII to call a Council, the election of a Polish pope, the resignation of Benedict XVI, or the election of Jorge Bergoglio, these acts were not anticipated. This capacity for surprise is itself an extraordinary sign of an office that is alive. Whatever historical forces and personalities shape the papacy—as an office and a person—it belongs ultimately to the Spirit. This is why it guides the church and is at her service.

The interview is a new and developing form of papal communication. It allows the personality as well as the teaching and opinions of the pope to emerge. It is well suited to Francis and his desire to be in dialogue with the church and the world. What is refreshing in his recent interview with Jesuit publications is the sense of immediacy, openness, and the person that is present throughout.

The genre and medium allow for a conversation that is both dynamic and evolving. Its style models a different genre in episcopal and magisterial speaking and relating. Nevertheless, it offers a deep, strong but gentle call for change—perhaps *conversion* is a better word—both in the present ecclesial culture as well as in the secular world. It is all the more challenging because it is an invitation to transform that does not simply rehearse negativities, but presents us with a renewed vision of possibilities, of hope. These are not grounded so much in a formal theological system as in a profound vision of a dynamic, compassionate, and merciful God, whose love embraces all humanity, especially the poor, despised, and undervalued. Francis speaks of and seeks to live out an incarnate love made intimate, real, and personal in Jesus Christ, a holy love in the "hidden sanctity" of ordinary lives. He speaks not so much as a teacher, but as a witness to what he has seen and experienced.

In contrast to the church as "resident alien," the pope offers a striking image of the church as "field hospital." This is not a church that is inwardly focused, reconciled to its own marginality almost as a Donatist badge of honor, or that obsesses about its own purity, inclined to substitute juridical observance for holiness. This is a church in love with women and men, deeply attentive to their needs— the cry of souls as well as bodies. It is a church that knows that it too lives purely from this overwhelming grace of God's love and mercy and even in its own weakness moves with humility to the service of humanity.

Although he does not use the image, one can see here the church of the "good Samaritan," a church that is not bound by cultural or theological systems, but without losing its identity, can reach out to a suffering world looking neither for recognition nor success. In a sense, it is the beautiful, graced, and sacred gesture of healing that Galway Kinnell describes in the poem "Saint Francis and the Sow":

> sometimes it is necessary
> to reteach a thing its loveliness . . .
> and retell it in words and in touch
> it is lovely

Such a church that reaches to put a "hand on the creased forehead of the sow" is not afraid to enter into dialogue or to change for the sake of Christ and his mission; not only is it a pastoral church, but a generative one—a Mother (and Father). In its reaching out this church rediscovers its own "loveliness," the mystery at its heart, the unfathomable fountain of life from which it lives. It experiences itself as the sacrament of salvation.

Throughout the interview one is struck by the delicacy and respect the pope shows for all persons, whom he tries to see first as women and men loved by the Lord before they are distorted by social, moral, economic, and political classifications. There is a balance and freedom here that is both attractive and creatively disturbing precisely because it asks us to see first without our categories.

Yet the interview moves at another level that is at least as challenging, if not more so. It is both subtle and profound; one might call it the personal human narrative and Jesuit subtext of love and change before the immensity of God's majesty— the *Deus semper maior*—an inexhaustible and incomprehensible love before which we can only kneel in humility, adoration, and loving service (*Spiritual Exercises* 114).

One familiar with the *Spiritual Exercises* cannot help but notice the way in which the whole of Pope Francis's understanding of himself and his mission as Bishop of Rome is rooted in and shaped by the *Spiritual Exercises* of St. Ignatius. There can be no genuine Jesuit or Christian life unless it is lived out of gratitude for the compassion and saving mercy we receive from the Father in the life, passion, death, and resurrection of his Son. This foundational experiential knowledge is the fruit of the first week of the Exercises. It is not just one transforming moment of realization and "conversion," though often it begins that way. It is the habitual knowledge that informs each moment of our lives, not as a paralyzing sense of guilt or shame, but as joyous thankfulness; an ever deepening self-knowledge of one's dependency and poverty combined with a liberating wonder; the experience of the depth of our sin, but the even greater immensity of God's saving love.

In all that Francis has said and done since his election as pope, it is clear that this is how he knows himself. His confession that he is a sinner is neither ritual nor formula; it is inscribed in his daily life and actions. Yet it gives him a sense of freedom, because it allows him to live always from the infinity of the Lord's compassionate mercy and embrace. He also knows, personally, that there is here too the gift of freedom—freedom to change, freedom to live beyond the preoccupations of self, in service of the greater need and suffering we encounter in those around us and in our crucified world and planet. And there is urgency. It is God's own urgency that searches for us and calls us to another way of being and acting and loving: to follow Christ in his poverty and humility and in his self-surrendering gift (*Spiritual Exercises* 167).

But we do not find this way except by loving Him. Nothing is more life-giving to us, to the church, and to the world; nothing is more countercultural.

So I find this interview both inspiring and deeply challenging. Francis is not afraid to speak about his sinfulness, his failures and how he has changed and continues to do so in order to be of ever greater service in the mission of the Lord. That speaks to us all, personally and ecclesially.

Although there is a freshness to his words and actions, he has said nothing new. Yet his desire to refocus and rebalance us on the dynamic economy of God's saving love "laboring and working in all things," as St. Ignatius says in the *Spiritual Exercises,* is not just about style; it is about substance. In a simple, direct, personal way he is presenting us with the reality of a God who does not condemn the world, but loves it more than it can believe or imagine (John 3:16–17). A God who can enter into the depths of our suffering is not repulsed by our woundedness or disfigurements, but who meets us wherever and whoever we are, heals us by bringing us ever closer to himself.

The danger of our cultural battles is that we forget the greatness and the richness of our tradition and its understanding not only of God, but also of humanity. Francis is reminding us of both— the God who is always the greater love and who calls us into an ever deeper community of loving responsibility for each other and our planet. As in the *Spiritual Exercises,* so in the evangelical message of Pope Francis we are invited to renew our response in person and as a church: "This is to ask for what I desire. Here it will be to ask for an intimate knowledge of the many blessings received, that filled with gratitude for all, I may in all things love and serve the Divine Majesty" (*Spiritual Exercises* 233).

James Hanvey, SJ, *a member of the British Province of the Society of Jesus, is Fellow in Theology at Campion Hall, Oxford.*

The Work of a Christian Lifetime

The Hard-Earned Insights of Pope Francis

Richard Rohr, OFM

FROM THE MOMENT he took the right name (I could not resist, dear Jesuits!), we knew something was different and even good. But little could we have imagined! Maybe we *did* have to go to "the ends of the earth," as he himself said after his election as pope, to find such an extraordinary and compelling man as Jorge Bergoglio. One popular TV host even said, "He is threatening my time slot!"

There are so many things I would like to say, but let me limit my remarks to one dimension of the pope's interview. Apart from the accolades he is receiving from the world press for his warmth, courage, and attitude of servanthood, Pope Francis has become for many of us a living example of the very healthy fruits of the "discernment of spirits" that Paul speaks of (1 Cor. 12:10) and the Society of Jesus has so skillfully unpackaged for the church universal.

The result is a subtlety that we have not come to expect from members of the church's hierarchy, an intelligence that is nondualistic and contemplative, an amazing courage that could only be sustained by very real prayer, and a compassion that has become a challenge and inspiration to all of us. Pope Francis is not dismissing the old, but like all true prophets he is revealing what the Big Tradition was really saying all along. Looking at much of our Catholic past, I can only think of Jesus's words to the people of Jerusalem: "How often have I desired to gather your children together as a hen gathers her brood under her wings, and you were not willing" (Matt. 23:37). Now we cannot get enough of it! We have a pope who gathers instead of scatters (Luke 11:23).

As a teacher of contemplative prayer and the contemplative mind, I have come to believe that the Western church has put far too much effort and fight into metaphysics ("what certainly is") and not nearly enough energy into practical epistemology ("How do you know what you think you know about what certainly is?"). This has made most of us victims of our own temperament, prejudices, culture, and prior agendas, while presuming we are speaking for the truly catholic. I have always felt that *Roman* and *catholic* were a bit of an oxymoron. Far too often it has been our small minds' understanding and very recent traditions that have had to pass for "what eternally is." ~~Ironically, it is Pope Francis's ability to critique his own mind ("discernment") that enables him to trust his own experience, while also balancing it with Scripture and Tradition~~. This is the big payoff that we Catholics have not granted to most Christians and that has allowed us to use Scripture and Tradition in such a wooden and mechanical way.

The Gospels caution us in this very regard. "Pay attention to how you listen" (Luke 8:18), Jesus says as he describes the different kinds of soil that receive the word of God (developmental theorists should love Jesus). ~~Pope Francis is emerging as a giant corrective to so much of our small seeing and listening by telling us that the first Christian hearing aid and lens through which we receive the moment must always be nothing less than the ears and eyes of love~~. It is almost too simple, and yet, as we have all learned, it is the hard work of a whole Christian lifetime. Pope Francis appears to be the work of art that emerges after a whole Christian lifetime. The world loves to look at it.

In case you think these thoughts are without due reference or merely my ideas, let me quote from his now famous interview. You will see for yourself and from the man himself. This, I believe, is the great tradition of our saints, mystics, and prophets, now spoken by a pope in the *America* interview:

Yes, in this quest to seek and find God in all things there is still an area of uncertainty. There must be. If a person says that he met God with total certainty and is not touched by a margin of uncertainty, then this is not good. For me, this is an important key. If one has the answers to all the questions—that is the proof that God is not with him. It means that he is a false prophet using religion for himself. The great leaders of the people of God, like Moses, have always left room for doubt. You must leave room for the Lord, not for our certainties; we must be humble. Uncertainty is in every true discernment that is open to finding confirmation in spiritual consolation.

The risk in seeking and finding God in all things, then, is the willingness to explain too much, to say with human certainty and arrogance, "God is here." We will find only a god that fits our measure. The correct attitude is that of St. Augustine: seek God to find him, and find God to keep searching for God forever.

Richard Rohr, OFM, *is the author of many books of spirituality, including* Falling Upward: A Spirituality for the Two Halves of Life.

$\mathcal{A}$n Ongoing Conversation

Additional Questions for Pope Francis

Rev. Robert P. Imbelli

IN THE 1950s, when I made my initial overtures toward classical music, there was no shortage of legendary orchestra conductors. But two stood at the summit of the pantheon: the Italian Arturo Toscanini and the German Wilhelm Furtwängler. It was said of Toscanini that he began a piece with its musical "logic" firmly established in his mind, and the execution became a seamless unfolding of that logic. In contrast, Furtwängler's style resembled an ongoing conversation among players and parts, gradually building toward a dramatic, sometimes surprising, conclusion.

Pope Francis's invocation of Furtwängler in his now much commented upon interview rekindled that old memory. Francis's preferential option for "narrative," "discernment," and the "mystical" seems more in harmony with the German conductor than with the Italian. Paradoxically, the style of his German predecessor, Benedict XVI, with his emphasis on *logos,* seems more attuned to Toscanini. Of course, both conductors (as both popes) respect and serve the same canonical texts. The notes are the same, though the accents and rhythms may noticeably vary.

Antonio Spadaro, SJ, met three times with Pope Francis and skillfully wove the pope's words into an integral whole. In his introductory remarks Father Spadaro makes this observation: "It is clear that Pope Francis is more used to having conversations than to giving lectures (*abituato più alla conversazione che alla lezione*)." And in his concluding reflections Father Spadaro opines: "Our time together was, in truth, more a conversation than an interview (*in realtà una conversazione più che un' intervista*)."

I think it important to recall these comments, because placing the pope's remarks in the genre of conversation may serve as a better guide for their ongoing interpretation. The conversation transpired between two believers, two fellow Jesuits, who share a commitment, vision, and common language. However, it is being overheard by a world avid to detect any hint of change in church teaching, but that is often deaf to the deeper language of faith. Thus, we see the predictable fixation by the secular media upon the issues of abortion and gay marriage—the very subjects that they charge portions of the hierarchy with obsessing over.

As many have already noted, Pope Francis does not dispute what has become settled magisterial teaching in this regard. "The teaching of the church," he insists, "is clear, and I am a son of the church." Significant, however, is his repositioning of these moral teachings in relation to the heart of the matter, which is the church's proclamation of the good news that "Jesus Christ has saved you!" Though he does not use the term here, it seems evident that what Francis discerns to be the pressing need of our time is a "new evangelization," a renewed proclamation of the love and mercy of God embodied and made available in Jesus Christ.

Here one appreciates the pope's striking evocation of the mystical dimension of Christian life. Like Benedict XVI, Francis insists that Christianity cannot be reduced to a moral code. It is preeminently about relationship with a person: the person of Jesus Christ. Thus, his contention that St. Ignatius of Loyola (who figures prominently in this conversation between two Jesuits) is not in the first instance an ascetic, but a mystic, and that the much praised Ignatian practice of discernment is not a technique mechanically applied, but "an instrument of struggle in order to know the Lord and follow him more closely."

Here too we can situate the pope's challenging presentation of Blessed Peter Faber as a model. What is compelling about Faber is his ability to join "interior experience, dogmatic expression, and structural reform" in an inseparable unity. As with Faber, so with Francis.

But the pope's insistence on the centrality of Jesus Christ, on discernment for the sake of discipleship, on Faber as exemplary in his ability to integrate inseparable components of church life, risks being ignored by the media's narrow focus on "hot-button issues." Thus, though this fraternal conversation is fascinating and winning, when transposed into the exclusively secular horizon of the pressroom, the words can be easily traduced.

If *America* were to commission me for a follow-up conversation with Pope Francis, here are some of the concerns I would raise.

Holy Father, in the first conversation you seem more critical of "restorationists" and "legalists" than of "relativists" (who so troubled your illustrious predecessor). You do briefly refer to "relativism," only to posit that the God of the Bible, whom we encounter on the journey (*nel cammino*), transcends relativism. I think the many eavesdroppers on the conversation would profit greatly from further elucidation of your thinking in this regard. How can we speak today of the God revealed in Jesus Christ as "absolute"?

You also issue a powerful call to the Society that bears Jesus's name to be "de-centered" from itself and ever centered upon "Christ and his church." But what are the implications of claiming Christ as center? Does it not impel us beyond narrative to engage questions of truth, beyond practice to its contemplative foundation? Having followed your homilies at Santa Marta on the Letter to the Colossians, proclaiming Christ as "the image of the invisible God" in whom "all things hold together" (Col. 1:15–17), I can certainly anticipate your response. But your further reflections on this theme would much enrich and challenge the continuing conversation, especially among those standing in the courtyard of the gentiles.

Related to this last point, you express your strong preference for "hope" rather than "optimism." But, probably for lack of time, you do not describe that hope to any extent, save to speak of it as a "theological virtue" and "ultimately a gift from God." I know that a world often devoid of hope (and even of optimism) longs to know the dimensions and reach of that hope and to hear an account (*logos*) of the hope that is in us.

Finally, at the close of your conversation, Father Spadaro posed a question about changes in human self-understanding over the centuries. You endorsed his point and instanced works of art from different historical periods to illustrate the fact. At the same time, as an astute spiritual director, you admit that men and women are often prone to self-deception. May I urge that we would all derive considerable profit from a further conversation that sets forth those principles that can guide our discernment of what constitutes authentic human flourishing. For, as I remind my own students, "finding God in all things" is the fruit of the first three weeks of Ignatius's *Spiritual Exercises*, not the point of departure.

Holy Father, despite your pronounced preference for Furtwängler, I trust you will not find these concerns of a Toscanini devotee misplaced. As you have often suggested, the Holy Spirit is found best in the blended harmony of voices.

Rev. Robert P. Imbelli, *a priest of the archdiocese of New York, teaches theology at Boston College. He was on the founding committee of Cardinal Joseph Bernardin's Catholic Common Ground Initiative.*

One Human Family

The Pope's Radical Call to Community

Meghan J. Clark

WHEN POPE FRANCIS decided to live at Santa Marta, the Vatican guesthouse, instead of the traditional papal apartment in the Apostolic Palace, many lauded him for his simplicity and rejection of perceived luxury. While he is indeed a humble man, Francis gives another reason for his decision to remain at Santa Marta: his yearning for a strong sense of community. "I cannot live without people. I need to live my life with others."

Francis bears testimony to this interpersonal spirituality not only in his words, but in his visits around Italy. In his interview, we find more evidence that this is simply authentic Francis; in his openness he offers an invitation to respond to the gospel and to be more fully human. In August, Pope Francis visited the Jesuit Refugee Center in Rome. Standing with the refugees, many of them fleeing horrific violence, he stated, "To serve means to work alongside the neediest, first of all to establish a close human relationship with them, based on solidarity. *Solidarity—this word elicits fear in the developed world. They try not to say it. It is almost a dirty word for them. But it's our word!" Our word*. The Holy Father reminds us in many of his speeches that *solidarity* is our word, but he is also continuously pushing us beyond the comforts of our religious boundaries to encounter the one human family.

Reflecting on the need to "think with the church," Francis beautifully situates the community that is the people of God: "In the history of salvation, God has saved a people. There is no full identity without belonging to a people. No one is saved alone, as an isolated individual, but God attracts us looking at the complex web of relationships that take place in the human community. God enters into this dynamic, this participation in the web of human relationships." This reminder that we are one human family and we are called into relationship with God and neighbor is very much needed in our time. A radical element of Catholicism, as Thomas Aquinas noted, is that we are called by God for union with God, for friendship with God, and that friendship with God requires loving our neighbor.

This interview is not out of character for Pope Francis, who has shown a remarkable degree of openness and intimacy since he was elected. His recognition that my humanity is bound up with his and with those suffering in poverty is the pastoral message America needs most today. We have a crisis of community, evidenced by the fact that the House of Representatives recently voted to cut $4 billion from the Supplemental Nutrition Assistance Program. Can we really say *solidarity* is "our word" when our country is so individualistic that we do not feel a moral responsibility to feed the hungry? The gospel and Pope Francis remind us that Christ entered into our *community* by becoming vulnerable and going to the margins.

Meghan J. Clark *is assistant professor of moral theology at St. John's University in Jamaica, New York.*

Mercy-ing

Kerry Weber

BEFORE THE ARTICLES in the national newspapers, before the talk-show appearances by our editors, before the debates in the blogosphere, there was the galley. The words that would receive worldwide attention from the media and would mark a milestone in Francis's papacy first came across my desk clearly printed on a few sheets of paper, just like any other article submitted to our magazine. Upon the arrival of these pages, I immediately sat down to proofread the text. To my surprise, the mundane (and occasionally dreaded) task of proofreading soon transformed into a truly prayerful experience. As I read the interview, I let it move me. I read slowly and found myself drawing an occasional smiley face in the margins alongside my corrections and trying to keep an occasional tear from smearing the ink.

I was struck by the overwhelming love that underscored so much of what Pope Francis said. I was also moved by the very fact that the pope had agreed to the interview, and that he had taken care to speak with the sort of honesty and charity that encourages the larger church to do the same. His description of the church as a "home of all" and his urging not to reduce it to "a nest protecting our mediocrity" serve as a call for each of us to look truthfully at how well we welcome others and how much we think of ourselves.

Francis's pastoral nature is clear, his desire to see people first—"individual persons, one at a time." He is, it seems, intent on making sure we know that his role, the role of the papacy, is not one in which he directs an anonymous church from on high, but one that allows him to journey alongside each of us toward Christ. He will not let us forget that he is one of us, a sinner. Nor will he let us forget that we, along with him, are redeemed through God's mercy.

Yet this mercy, Francis reminds us, is not simply a grace requested in supplication and passively received. It is a motivating force, furthering the work of our church. "[T]he ministers of the church must be ministers of mercy above all," Francis said. This is not a request from which we can opt out. Mercy, in Francis's church, calls us, allows us, requires us to become better. And it is a call to all people of goodwill. But how should we begin? How do we accompany others in mercy, a quality difficult to define and even more difficult to live authentically?

The answer, perhaps, can be found in a wonderfully invented word from Pope Francis: *mercy-ing*. In turning the noun into a verb, a sentiment into an action, Francis calls us not only to have mercy or to show mercy, but to *embody* mercy. The word emphasizes the active element of mercy, as a force that binds us, compels us, and enables us to love one another more fully.

This call for *mercy-ing* is at once a call for humility and a call to greatness. It pushes us to live out the extraordinary gospel message, to acknowledge the dignity of our fellow travelers on this journey and the reality of our own faults. It is a call to look toward Christ and then look inward before we respond to others. It is a call to allow ourselves to be moved, to proceed deliberately, with compassion alongside our corrections. In short, *mercy-ing* is a call to listen to one another with love. It allows us to realize the power of words clearly and lovingly spoken, and of the Word humbly lived.

Kerry Weber *is managing editor of* America *and the author of* Mercy in the City: How to Feed the Hungry, Give Drink to the Thirsty, Visit the Imprisoned, and Keep Your Day Job *(Loyola Press).*

The Accessible Pope

Spiritual Sensitivity, Understanding, Tolerance, and a Thoughtful, Rich Sensibility

Margot Patterson

THERE IS SUCH excitement today about Pope Francis, among Catholics and non-Catholics alike. Just a few nights ago at an informal dinner I met two Protestant ministers who expressed this excitement, their belief that this pope could issue in something fresh and different in the world. As a Catholic, I share this enthusiasm for the new pope, who has not put one foot wrong publicly since assuming the papacy and who is instead surprising us with how genuine, warm, and at ease with himself he appears. He is not captured by his new position or hemmed in by protocol, and he has that rare quality all leaders would wish for: the common touch.

Listening to the first news reports about the papal interview and the pope's comment on the need for the church to focus more on the pastoral needs of the people and less on hot-button topics like abortion and gay marriage, I felt a sense of relief that perhaps now U.S. bishops would lessen their fixation on these polarizing issues, a fixation that has not yielded any tangible results. I thought the pope's striking analogy of the church as a field hospital—where one must treat the wounded and tend to the most serious injuries first, rather than asking people about their cholesterol levels—to be a brilliant way of capturing the danger of the church falling casualty to its dogma and very revealing of Pope Francis's great ability to communicate.

Reading the entire interview in *America,* I come away further impressed by the pope's humility and openness. His description of what he thinks the Society of Jesus should be--"searching, creative, and generous"—sounds just like what he is himself. His emphasis on collegiality and consultation seems very positive for the church in its relations with other Christian churches, particularly the Orthodox, and for the church in dialogue with the different elements (sometimes, frankly, factions) within it. His words about strengthening the presence of women in the church were encouraging to me, and to many other women, I am sure.

When he speaks of the church as the totality of the people of God, both the pastors and the people, and of striking a new balance between the moral and dogmatic teachings of the church, I feel sure all of this will be very popular with Catholics in the United States. I am struck by how well he puts it too, in language that evokes the ineffability and grace of the Christian message: "We have to find a new balance; otherwise even the moral edifice of the church is likely to fall like a house of cards, losing the freshness and fragrance of the gospel. The proposal of the gospel must be more simple, profound, radiant. It is from this proposition that the moral consequences then flow."

I can hardly not be interested in what the pope has to say about the government of the church. And how can I not be heartened by the fact that he seems flexible, open-minded, and aware of the need for the church to move forward? I am, and yet it is not the pope's comments about church government that most engage me in the interview. More interesting to me is his discussion of himself, his comparison of himself with Matthew in the painting *The Calling of St. Matthew* by Caravaggio, his comments on art and culture, his discussion of discernment and the importance of magnanimity. I am fascinated too by his mention of "the lurking danger of living in a laboratory." He contrasts this with the frontier, where we need to live. "I am afraid of laboratories, because in the laboratory you take the problems and then you bring them home to tame them, to paint them artificially, out of their context," Pope Francis says. "You cannot bring home the frontier, but you have to live on the border and be audacious."

This call to live creatively, in the real world, not to be captured by the simplicity of abstract ideas and solutions, seems to me an insight I do not hear very often. We have to remember it to be human. It is the power of abstract ideas that turns us into ideologues. I am sure Pope Francis's remarks about being a sinner surprised some people, probably because sin does not seem very real to many people these days. We have problems, complexes, issues that need to be straightened out, and all these are treated as if they are outside ourselves, something to be regulated like a thermostat or cured with a round of antibiotics. It is a different mind-set from "the adventure of the quest for meeting God," which is innately uncertain, as Francis says.

Spiritual sensitivity, understanding, tolerance, and a thoughtful, rich sensibility are what one seeks in a priest, a pontiff (and, incidentally, a friend), and Pope Francis clearly possesses these traits in full. That he is commanding so much attention is excellent. One wants a pope to be able to influence people. After reading what Pope Francis has to say about writers and artists he likes, I am now tempted to read Hölderlin, Borges, and Alessandro Manzoni and see *La Strada* again. I would probably want to call the pope to discuss them after I did, but that is not a bad thing either, especially as these days there is a chance he might call me back.

There are probably risks in being accessible, but this pope's accessibility is part of what is making him seem remarkable.

Margot Patterson, *columnist for* America, *has written for a variety of newspapers and magazines in the United States and abroad. Most recently, she worked for* The National Catholic Reporter *for seven years as senior writer and then opinion and arts editor.*

The Pope's Interview and the Bible

"That Finger of Jesus, Pointing at Matthew. That's Me."

John W. Martens

IN THE MAGNIFICENT interview Antonio Spadaro, SJ, conducted with Pope Francis for *America*, many aspects of the pope's life and mind emerged. Particularly interesting to me were the ways in which Scripture lies as a foundation for his pattern of life and mind. Scripture was not often quoted in the interview; in some ways, I believe, because of how substantial it is as groundwork for who he is. All popes are immersed in the gospel, and each of them focuses on particular aspects of the gospel in how they live and in what they teach, which is not to say they ignore the rest, just that all of us have habits of mind. I want to focus on two passages of Scripture that did surface as bedrock for this pope, one explicitly and one implicitly.

In the section "Who Is Jorge Mario Bergoglio?" Pope Francis speaks of the call of St. Matthew from the Gospel of Matthew, the only Gospel that uses the name of Matthew in the call (Mark 2:14 and Luke 5:27 have the same scene, but name the man Levi). The actual call is short, one verse:

> As Jesus was walking along, he saw a man called Matthew sitting at the tax booth; and he said to him, "Follow me." And he got up and followed him. (9:9)

It is a minimal account, but it is what follows in Matthew 9:10–13 (and beyond) that gives it context (again, the same context is offered in Mark 2:15–17 and Luke 5:29–32 with the dinner at Levi's house):

> As Jesus was walking along, he saw a man called Matthew sitting at the tax booth; and he said to him, "Follow me." And he got up and followed him. And as he sat at dinner in the house, many tax-collectors and sinners came and were sitting with him and his disciples. When the Pharisees saw this, they said to his disciples, "Why does your teacher eat with tax-collectors and sinners?" But when he heard this, he said, "Those who are well have no need of a physician, but those who are sick. Go and learn what this means, 'I desire mercy, not sacrifice.' For I have come to call not the righteous but sinners." (9:9–13)

Before examining the passage, listen to what the pope says about it in the context of Caravaggio's painting of the scene:

I do not know Rome well. I know a few things. These include the Basilica of St. Mary Major; I always used to go there. I know St. Mary Major, St. Peter's . . . but when I had to come to Rome, I always stayed in [the neighborhood of] Via della Scrofa. From there I often visited the Church of St. Louis of France, and I went there to contemplate the painting of *The Calling of St. Matthew,* by Caravaggio.

That finger of Jesus, pointing at Matthew. That's me. I feel like him. Like Matthew. It is the gesture of Matthew that strikes me: he holds on to his money as if to say, "No, not me! No, this money is mine." Here, this is me, a sinner on whom the Lord has turned his gaze. And this is what I said when they asked me if I would accept my election as pontiff. I am a sinner, but I trust in the infinite mercy and patience of our Lord Jesus Christ, and I accept in a spirit of penance.

In placing himself in the role of sinner called by God, Pope Francis not only places himself in the role of the Apostle Matthew, but that of every person, all of whom are sinners and all of whom are called by God. In identifying, though, with the sinner he also identifies with Jesus's mission to call all people to receive God's mercy without exception. When Jesus ate with "many tax-collectors and sinners," identifying with these outcasts, the religious experts of the day, the Pharisees—and they were both expert and righteous in many respects—were upset: "Why does your teacher eat with tax-collectors and sinners?" Jesus's response is: "Those who are well have no need of a physician, but those who are sick. Go and learn what this means, 'I desire mercy, not sacrifice.' For I have come to call not the righteous but sinners."

In identifying with the sinners Pope Francis classifies his primary identity as a person who has been saved by God's mercy not as a religious expert. He also identifies the primary mission of the church as reaching out to "those who are sick," to offer healing to all those in need, modern-day "tax-collectors and sinners" who might not previously have found a place at the table. This is the act of extending mercy to all.

This leads to the implicit identification of another Gospel passage in the section "The Church as Field Hospital," though the imagery builds on Matthew 9:9–13 (and parallels) as well, and that is the parable of the Good Samaritan, found in Luke 10:25–37:

Just then a lawyer stood up to test Jesus. "Teacher," he said, "what must I do to inherit eternal life?" He said to him, "What is written in the law? What do you read there?" He answered, "You shall love the Lord your God with all your heart, and with all your soul, and with all your strength, and with all your mind; and your neighbor as yourself." And he said to him, "You have given the right answer; do this, and you will live."

But wanting to justify himself, he asked Jesus, "And who is my neighbor?" Jesus replied, "A man was going down from Jerusalem to Jericho, and fell into the hands of robbers, who stripped him, beat him, and went away, leaving him half dead. Now by chance a priest was going down that road; and when he saw him, he passed by on the other side. So likewise a Levite, when he came to the place and saw him, passed by on the other side. But a Samaritan while traveling came near him; and when he saw him, he was moved with pity. He went to him and bandaged his wounds, having poured oil and wine on them. Then he put him on his own animal, brought him to an inn, and took care of him. The next day he took out two denarii, gave them to the innkeeper, and said, 'Take care of him; and when I come back, I will repay you whatever more you spend.' Which of these three, do you think, was a neighbor to the man who fell into the hands of the robbers?" He said, "The one who showed him mercy." Jesus said to him, "Go and do likewise."

Again, before examining the passage, here is what Pope Francis said about the church as field hospital:

I see clearly that the thing the church needs most today is the ability to heal wounds and to warm the hearts of the faithful; it needs nearness, proximity. I see the church as a field hospital after battle. It is useless to ask a seriously injured person if he has high cholesterol and about the level of his blood sugars! You have to heal his wounds. Then we can talk about everything else. Heal the wounds, heal the wounds. . . . And you have to start from the ground up.

The church sometimes has locked itself up in small things, in small-minded rules. The most important thing is the first proclamation: Jesus Christ has saved you. And the ministers of the church must be ministers of mercy above all. The confessor, for example, is always in danger of being either too much of a rigorist or too lax. Neither is merciful, because neither of them really takes responsibility for the person. The rigorist washes his hands so that he leaves it to the commandment. The loose minister washes his hands by simply saying, "This is not a sin" or something like that. In pastoral ministry we must accompany people, and we must heal their wounds. . . .

A person once asked me, in a provocative manner, if I approved of homosexuality. I replied with another question: "Tell me, when God looks at a gay person, does he endorse the existence of this person with love, or reject and condemn this person?" We must always consider the person. Here we enter into the mystery of the human being. In life, God accompanies persons, and we must accompany them, starting from their situation. It is necessary to accompany them with mercy. When that happens, the Holy Spirit inspires the priest to say the right thing.

The Good Samaritan stands as the most likely passage behind this section due to the emphasis on "heal the wounds, heal the wounds" of the "seriously injured person." "We must heal their wounds," said Francis, and "we must accompany them, starting from their situation. It is necessary to accompany them with mercy."

The Samaritan comes across a man beaten on the road in Jesus's parable, and he does not ask, "How did you get yourself in this situation?" or "What did you do to deserve this?" or "Who are you, a Samaritan or a Jew?" At personal risk to himself, since the robbers could still be present, the Samaritan helps the unknown man without any idea of the situation that led to this event or of the man's identity. Note again, the religious experts do not stop and help, since they might have pressing responsibilities in the Temple, where priests and Levites serve the sacrificial system. This is not an indictment, however, of the Jewish religious elite or the Temple service; it is an indictment of any religious elite that would place sacrifice over mercy. Remember Jesus's command from Matthew 9:13: "Go and learn what this means, 'I desire mercy, not sacrifice.'" The Good Samaritan parable puts into practice Jesus's command to learn what "I desire mercy, not sacrifice" means, for at the end of the parable Jesus asks the lawyer, a religious expert himself, which person had acted like a neighbor in this parable. The lawyer answers, "The one who showed him mercy." Jesus says to him, "Go and do likewise."

In his words and in his actions, Pope Francis has identified with the sinners and the desire to "Go and do likewise." He sees the church's primary purpose as showing abundant mercy to those who are hurt, wounded, and lost, because that mercy and healing is what he has experienced— "That finger of Jesus, pointing at Matthew. That's me"—and because that is what Jesus commanded his disciples to do. As Pope Francis continued:

> Proclamation in a missionary style focuses on the essentials, on the necessary things: this is also what fascinates and attracts more, what makes the heart burn, as it did for the disciples at Emmaus. We have to find a new balance; otherwise even the moral edifice of the church is likely to fall like a house of cards, losing the freshness and fragrance of the gospel. The proposal of the gospel must be more simple, profound, radiant. It is from this proposition that the moral consequences then flow.

There is a third biblical reference there, Emmaus, from Luke 24, in which Jesus appears to his downtrodden disciples, walking and talking with them, unbeknownst to them. When they recognize who it is, that it is Jesus, they say, "Were not our hearts burning within us while he was talking to us on the road, while he was opening the scriptures to us?" (24:32). To recognize Jesus, though, you need an encounter, and for that you need an introduction. Mercy seems like a good way to introduce people to Jesus.

John W. Martens *is associate professor of theology at the University of St. Thomas in St. Paul, Minnesota, where he teaches early Christianity and Judaism. He also writes "The Word" column for* America.

The People of God, at Long Last

Drew Christiansen, SJ

OF THE IMAGES of the church that emerged from the Second Vatican Council, the People of God was the most important and the most popular. For almost twenty years, it was a constant in the Catholic vocabulary, even entering into liturgy. But from the beginning, it was regarded as suspect. The late Cardinal Avery Dulles, SJ, in *Models of the Church* worried about its democratizing subtext. Others probably feared it as subversive of hierarchical authority. John Paul II neglected it, preferring the magisterial (institutional) model of the church, and sometimes even the teaching church seemed to be reduced to the pope alone.

For me the real news, potentially the most church-renewing news, in Pope Francis's interview is his revival of the understanding of the church as the People of God. "The image of the church I like," Pope Francis told Father Spadaro, "is that of the holy, faithful people of God. . . . There is no full identity without belonging to a people. No one is saved alone, as an isolated individual, but God attracts us looking at the complex web of relationships that take place in the human community. God enters into this dynamic, this participation in the web of human relationships." This is "big tent" Catholicism, a church that welcomes all. No longer an institution or, worse, an office, the church is "a community," "a web of relationships." Francis embraces the model of the church that the late Cardinal Dulles called his own favorite, "a community of disciples."

Astoundingly, Francis identifies infallibility as inhering in the whole church: "a supernatural sense of the faith of all the people walking together. . . . ~~When the dialogue among the people and the bishops and the pope goes down this road and is genuine, then it is assisted by the Holy Spirit.~~" This is an entirely orthodox understanding of infallibility, but one sidelined in practice for too long in favor of a monarchical view. It is what Blessed John Henry Newman called "a conspiracy of bishops and faithful."

For me the other headline in the Francis interview is the refocusing of the church on the gospel. God's love is the center once more of the church's preaching. Morality has a place, but it is secondary to the gospel of God's love and mercy. To be sure, what Pope John Paul II called "the Gospel of Life" has a place in the church's proclamation, as it has had from the beginning. But it is not the central message, and what Pope Francis calls the "obsession" with sexual morality has distorted Catholic pastoral practice and social ministry, especially in the United States. "[T]he proclamation of the saving love of God comes before moral and religious imperatives," he told his interviewer. Popular response has already made obvious how people now hear the good news in the gospel once again. "New evangelization"? Pope Francis is the "new evangelization" personified.

Like the gospel of Jesus itself, the gospel Francis preaches also shows up the Pharisaism of the moral righteousness that seeks to establish public morality according to abstract norms without making pastoral allowance for context and persons. Can there be any convincing answer to his question, "Tell me, when God looks at a gay person, does he endorse the existence of this person with love, or reject and condemn this person?"

Drew Christiansen, SJ, *is former editor in chief of* America *and an expert in international affairs.*

Part Three

Praying with
a Big Heart

Praying with a Big Heart

Spiritual Reflections on the Papal Interview

James Martin, SJ

WE WERE DELIGHTED at *America* to publish the English-language translation of this moving interview with Pope Francis. Most readers of this book are aware of the astonishing worldwide response to the pope's words. Within minutes of the interview's release, every form of media leapt upon his comments as one of the biggest religion stories of the year. Much of the media's attention was focused on the pope's commentary on a variety of hot-button topics, such as reform of the church, homosexuality, contraception, and abortion. This is not surprising: it was seen as more newsworthy.

Somewhat overlooked were the profound spiritual insights hidden within the long interview, which the editors at *America* treasured as we slowly read over the transcript in the weeks preceding its publication. In fact, our review process was somewhere between editing and spiritual reading. One

editor said that it was the first time she found herself in tears over a galley.

A Big Heart Open to God is primarily a spiritual
testimony and, as such, represents an invitation to
prayer. So let me offer a few spiritual reflections on
selected quotes and suggest some reflection questions for your own personal prayer.

"I AM A SINNER WHOM THE
LORD HAS LOOKED UPON."

Many commentators focused on what was seen
as a remarkable admission for a pope. At the beginning of the conversation, Father Spadaro, who
conducted the interview on behalf of several Jesuit
journals, asks, "Who is Jorge Mario Bergoglio?"
The pope pauses for a moment and then answers,
"I am a sinner." He continues: "This is the most
accurate definition. It is not a figure of speech, a
literary genre. I am a sinner." That quote was the
focus of many stories written after the interview's
publication.

To me, however, it was not surprising that the
pope spoke of himself in that way. Truly holy men
and women fully understand their limitations and
their sinfulness—in a word, their humanity. So do
popes. Pope John Paul I, who served as pope for
only one month in 1978, once said, "I am only a
poor man, accustomed to small things and silence."
Both Pope John Paul II and Pope Benedict spoke in

a similar vein during their pontificates. Like all men and women close to God, in his bones Jorge Mario Bergoglio, SJ, knows that he is a sinner: ~~imperfect, flawed, and struggling~~.

But there was more to the interview than an admission of sinfulness, for Francis elaborates by saying, "I am a sinner whom the Lord has looked upon." For anyone familiar with Ignatian spirituality—the spirituality based on the life and writings of St. Ignatius Loyola, the sixteenth-century founder of the Jesuit order—those words were instantly recognizable. The more popular formulation of that idea is that a person is a ~~"loved sinner."~~

In Ignatian spirituality, this phrase finds its origins in the *Spiritual Exercises*, St. Ignatius Loyola's classic manual for prayer. At the beginning of the *Exercises* a person is asked to meditate on the blessings he or she has received from God. For most people, looking back on the graces that God has given them evokes tremendous gratitude.

In time, however, another movement becomes evident. Gradually, you become aware of your sinfulness. This does not mean that you see yourself as worthless or shameful. ~~Rather, in light of all the blessings God has poured out, you become conscious of the reality of the human condition: we are all flawed, limited, imperfect people.~~ As one spiritual director told me, ~~"In the bright sunshine~~

of God's love, you begin to see your shadow." Typically, you experience a sudden awareness that, in the face of your sinfulness, God still loves you. So you are a "loved sinner" or, as the pope says, "a sinner whom the Lord has looked upon." It is a highly important concept in the spiritual life.

Too often we focus only on one aspect of this reality. Either we see ourselves simply as sinners, unredeemed and unloved. Or we view ourselves simply as loved by God and in no need of looking at our sins. True Christian spirituality keeps these two realities present to one another. We are loved sinners.

For Reflection

1. Where has God blessed you?
2. What would you say is your core sin?
3. Can you see yourself as a "loved sinner"?

"DISCERNMENT TAKES TIME."

When asked what element of Ignatian spirituality most enables him to live out his ministry as pope, Francis had a one-word answer: *discernment*. As with a few concepts in Ignatian spirituality, the English word used masks a deeper reality.

In common parlance, a "discerning" person often is one who makes wise decisions or has good taste. In Catholic spiritual circles it means much more. In the Ignatian tradition, "discernment" is a way of prayerfully making decisions based on practices from the *Spiritual Exercises*. In fact, a great deal of St. Ignatius's great work is focused on making holy, healthy, and life-giving decisions. The original title of his text was *Spiritual Exercises to Overcome Oneself, and to Order One's Life, Without Reaching a Decision Through Some Disordered Affection.* In other words, these are exercises designed to help us make good and free decisions.

In the *Exercises,* Ignatius offers several techniques for doing so—though this is not the place for a long description of his type of discernment. But at the heart of Ignatian discernment is something simple: a belief not only that God wants us to make good decisions, but also that God will help us do so. Moreover, by paying attention to the various "movements" in our hearts we can come to understand God's desires for us. In the most basic application, when we are aligned with God's desires for us, we will feel a sense of rightness, what Ignatius calls "consolation." Over time, then, we can learn to ponder our choices, weigh these feelings, and search out God's desires.

But as Francis says, "Discernment takes time." At one point in the interview, the pope says bluntly, "I am always wary of the first decision, that is, the first thing that comes to my mind if I have to make a decision. This is usually the wrong thing. I have to wait and assess, looking deep into myself, taking the necessary time." Often there is no need to rush. Rather than trying to figure things out, it may be more helpful to ask God to reveal things to us.

Part of making good decisions is knowing yourself and guarding against unhealthy patterns of deciding—like rash, selfish, or angry decisions. The goal is freedom—the freedom to be open to God's voice.

For Reflection

1. What is the best decision you ever made?
2. Did you, or do you, feel a sense of "rightness" about that decision?
3. Can you see God as guiding you in that discernment process?

> "MY AUTHORITARIAN AND QUICK
> MANNER OF MAKING DECISIONS
> LED ME TO HAVE SERIOUS
> PROBLEMS AND TO BE ACCUSED
> OF BEING ULTRACONSERVATIVE."

This quote hardly seems like the most spiritual of reflections. It sounds more like a sentence from a business management textbook! Yet the pope's frank admission marks a spiritual moment in the interview, because it is an honest assessment of himself. It is an indication of humility.

Pope Francis is speaking of his time as a Jesuit regional superior (or "provincial") in Argentina in the 1970s, a tremendously difficult time for him, for the Argentinean people, and for Argentinean Jesuits. The pope is remarkably frank about what he sees as the failings of Jorge Mario Bergoglio, SJ, during that controversy-filled period.

In the interview he "accuses himself," as Jesuits sometimes say, of making rash and hasty decisions. Later, he returns to that theme, saying bluntly that he has realized that in his life the first decision he makes "is usually the wrong thing." Without delving into the choices that the pope made during his time as a Jesuit provincial (at the extremely young age of thirty-six, which he calls "crazy"), what strikes me most about this self-examination is its refreshing and almost embarrassing candor.

The former Jesuit provincial does not use the circumlocution "mistakes were made." Nor does he remark in an offhand way, "Things could have been done better." Instead, the pope offers a blunt assessment of himself as a Jesuit superior and an imperfect human being who "created problems." Part of the Jesuit spiritual tradition—indeed, the Christian spiritual tradition—is an "examination of conscience," or more generally an examination of one's moral activity. Here you can see the leader of the Catholic Church doing just that, in the most open manner imaginable—in a worldwide interview. Here is true humility.

Humility is the gateway to holiness. Without it, we place ourselves, rather than God, at the center of our lives. Without it, we rely on only ourselves without grasping our fundamental dependence on God. Without it, we are tempted to think of ourselves as perfect, and so we resist any opportunity for growth.

Where would Pope Francis be if he had resisted the invitation for self-examination? If he had resisted the call to humility? His blunt assessment of himself is an invitation for all of us humbly to examine our decisions and our actions.

For Reflection

1. How have you learned from your mistakes?
2. Can you ask God in prayer for greater self-knowledge?
3. In what areas of your life have you grown?

> "WE SHOULD NOT EVEN THINK,
> THEREFORE, THAT 'THINKING
> WITH THE CHURCH' MEANS
> ONLY THINKING WITH THE
> HIERARCHY OF THE CHURCH."

Here is something new, as far as I know. While the phrase "thinking with the church" may be unfamiliar to some readers, it is well known by Jesuits and Catholic scholars. In the *Spiritual Exercises*, St. Ignatius lays out his famous "Rules for Thinking [or

Feeling] with the Church," an invitation for a person to incorporate himself or herself deeply into the life of the church and align himself or herself in the most profound way with the church's teaching. It is a long list of suggestions, which mainly concern praising the church and supporting it. Perhaps the most famous dictum is that even if a person sees something as white, he or she should "believe it to be black" if the church determines it. That last phrase is often used as a warning—or a threat—against those who are seen as "not in line" with one or another church pronouncement. It is also used as an argument for blind obedience.

Pope Francis, as a former Jesuit novice director and provincial, knows the *Spiritual Exercises* exceedingly well. In the interview, the pope gives the expression "thinking with the church" a new interpretation. The church, says the pope, is the "totality of God's people," pastors and people together, not just the hierarchy. So thinking with the church, as he says, is not simply thinking with the hierarchy. In this we hear echoes of the Second Vatican Council's emphasis on the church not as a top-down organization, but something broader; in a beautiful phrase, the church is the "People of God."

Francis's understanding of "thinking with the church" is a more capacious definition than I have heard, certainly from a pope—and I am speaking not simply of recent popes, but popes since the time of St. Ignatius in the sixteenth century. Perhaps only Jorge Mario Bergoglio, a Jesuit who understands the *Spiritual Exercises* and who occupies the papacy, could say this, and even reinterpret Ignatius in the process.

For Catholics and Christians, this theological insight opens a variety of questions.

For Reflection

1. How do you see the Holy Spirit alive in the church today?
2. What does "thinking with the church" mean for you?
3. Are there times when you need to listen more carefully to what the church says?

"I SEE THE CHURCH AS A FIELD HOSPITAL AFTER BATTLE."

There are many images of the church. The church is the Body of Christ, as St. Paul said, the visible body of Christ on earth. It is the People of God, as the Second Vatican Council wrote, all of us—clergy and laity, saints and sinners, past and present—gathered together. It is our Holy Mother, an ancient image of a warm and maternal presence.

But until the pope used it, I had never heard the image of the church as a "field hospital." In

Pope Francis's imagination, the church is akin to a hospital caring for the wounded or the very sick in the midst of a war. The image came in response to a question about the various issues the church should most focus on. Pope Francis responded that rather than focusing on smaller matters, the church must turn its attention to larger ones. And so he says, "It is useless to ask a seriously injured person if he has high cholesterol and about the level of his blood sugars! You have to heal his wounds." In other words, first things first.

The metaphor is a beautiful one and moves us beyond simply thinking about what the hot-button issues of the day are. When I read those words, I thought of a hospital set in a field of battle, covered only by a tarpaulin or cloth held up by steel posts and open to the air. Inside were the people who most needed help. But also, in my imagination, I saw people coming in and going out freely. The church was open to all, and focused on helping those most in need. The church was providing what Pope John XXIII once called the "medicine of mercy."

Notice too that the church here is not a "warrior," though it is sometimes necessary to fight (and to suffer) for our beliefs. No, here the church is the group that cares for people wounded in the battles and struggles that come into the world. What is needed most today, said the pope, is a church that can "heal wounds" and "warm the hearts of the people."

For Reflection

1. How does Christ "heal wounds"?
2. How can you warm hearts?
3. What else does the image of the church as a field hospital say to you?

"IT IS NECESSARY TO ACCOMPANY THEM WITH MERCY."

During an in-flight press conference after World Youth Day in Rio de Janeiro in 2013, Pope Francis made headlines when he uttered the words, "Who am I to judge?" when asked a question about gay priests in the church.

At the time, several commentators opined that the pope's words were not only uninteresting (since the pope did not change any church teaching on homosexuality); they were also limited, applying only, they said, to gay priests. But in our interview, Francis speaks at some length about gay persons in general, and even notes that his comments during the in-flight press conference referred to gay persons, not simply gay priests: "During the return flight from Rio de Janeiro I said that if a homosexual person is of goodwill and is in search of God, I am no one to judge."

The new interview continues Francis's pastoral stance toward gays and lesbians. "We must always consider the person," he said. "Here we enter into the mystery of the human being. In life, God accompanies persons, and we must accompany them, starting from their situation. It is necessary to accompany them with mercy." While none of this changes church teaching, the pope's words have changed the way the church speaks to and about gay persons. And that is new.

But there is more to this comment than simply a commentary on gay and lesbian persons. It is much deeper than that. Pope Francis leads with mercy. Mercy has been a hallmark of his papacy from its earliest days. The interview in *America* reveals a gentle pastor who looks upon people as individuals, not as categories.

The pope also challenges us to reach out with mercy, as Jesus did, to those who are seen as on the margins. Remember that for Jesus there is no "other," no one to be shunned or excluded. When confronted with a Roman centurion, a woman suspected of adultery, or a person seen to be a notorious sinner, Jesus is merciful.

He is especially merciful to those who are sick or poor. Indeed, the English translation of what happens inside Jesus when he sees the poor or sick or hungry is this: "His heart went out to them."

The original Greek word used in the Gospels is much stronger: *splagchnizomai*. That long word means, literally, that Jesus's bowels were moved with emotion. This was the seat of the emotions for Greek-speaking people in the time of the Gospels. In other words, Jesus felt compassion, or mercy, *in his guts*.

This is the emotion that we are called to feel for one another: compassion, pity, mercy.

For Reflection

1. Are there people that you consider to be "other"?
2. Can you hear Jesus saying "Blessed are the merciful" to you?
3. Who in your life can you "accompany with mercy"?

"GOD IS FOUND IN THE GENTLE BREEZE PERCEIVED BY ELIJAH."

This is one of my favorite quotes in the entire interview. When asked a question about encountering God, Pope Francis refers to a passage from the Old Testament in which the prophet Elijah is listening for God's voice:

Now there was a great wind, so strong that it was splitting mountains and breaking rocks in pieces before the Lord, but the Lord was not in the wind; and after the wind an earthquake, but the Lord was not in the earthquake; and after the earthquake a fire, but the Lord was not in the fire; and after the fire a sound of sheer silence. When Elijah heard it, he wrapped his face in his mantle and went out and stood at the entrance of the cave. Then there came a voice to him that said, "What are you doing here, Elijah?" (1 Kings 19:11–13)

Elijah recognizes God not in great, dramatic events such as a tornado or an earthquake or a fire, but in what some translators call a "still, small voice" or "a gentle breeze."

This is not to say that God is not active in dramatic events in our lives—a wedding, a birth, a death—or in the Bible—a pillar of fire, a burning bush, a storm stilled. God is active *everywhere*. But it is human nature to concentrate so much on looking for God in the big things that we often do not look for God in the small. We all want the overwhelming epiphany, the unmistakably dramatic moment, when we can say, "Aha! Now that is really God!"

The pope reminds us that the smaller things in life—a smile on a baby's face, the sight of the sunlight on the pavement, and yes, a gentle breeze—are all ways in which we can experience God.

This is most often the way that we experience God—in what might be called our "ordinary time."

To help us recognize these moments, we need to cultivate a sense of awareness, so that our eyes are open. We also need trust, so that with open eyes we might believe that this is indeed, as Elijah perceived, God's voice.

For Reflection

1. What "gentle breezes" help you see God?
2. How can your ordinary time be extraordinary?
3. How can you notice God more in your day-to-day life?

"IN THIS QUEST TO SEEK AND FIND GOD IN ALL THINGS THERE IS STILL AN AREA OF UNCERTAINTY."

Over the past decades Christianity has been seen as a religion of certainty. And the true Christian is indeed certain of many things: God became human, Christ is risen, the Holy Spirit is with us. All of those things are at the heart of the Christian faith.

There is always the danger, however, that the Christian faith can tempt us into thinking that we know all there is to know about religion, spirituality, and God. But as much as we can know about God—through experience, through church tradition, through the Scriptures, and most of all through Jesus Christ—God remains essentially unknowable. If you can define it and categorize it, then what you have defined and categorized is not God. Most thoughtful believers would assent to this, but the temptation to complete certainty is always there, because most of us are uncomfortable with uncertainty.

Moreover, we may be tempted to believe that God can only work in certain ways, through certain people and at certain times. But the idea that God might be at work in other religions (one of the teachings of the Second Vatican Council) and in people who do not seem particularly religious (one of the teachings of Jesus of Nazareth) is essential, if we are to maintain a stance of humility before the Lord.

"If one has the answers to all the questions," says the pope, "that is the proof that God is not with him." Can we "live the question," as one of my spiritual directors once asked me? Can we remember that God is, to paraphrase the philosopher Gabriel Marcel, not a problem to be solved, but a mystery to be lived?

Be open to the mystery of God.

For Reflection

1. What is your favorite image of God?
2. Have you ever experienced God in a surprising place?
3. Are you open to living a mystery?

"I HAVE A DOGMATIC CERTAINTY: GOD IS IN EVERY PERSON'S LIFE."

Pope Francis is comfortable with gray. In the interview, he speaks out against what he calls a "doctrinal 'security'" and offers a gentle critique of those who "stubbornly try to recover a past that no longer exists." Pope Francis asks us to move away from a church that "locked itself up in small things, in small-minded rules." Instead, he invites the church deeper into the world of uncertainty, which is where most of us live anyway.

This is the world in which Jesus of Nazareth walked: the real world, in which people experienced uncertainty and confronted the need to make decisions. It is the milieu of the everyday believer. Jesus entered this world in first-century Palestine, and the church must be comfortable in that same world today.

But there is one thing of which Pope Francis is sure: "I have a dogmatic certainty: God is in every person's life. God is in everyone's life. Even if the life of a person has been a disaster, even if it is destroyed by vices, drugs, or anything else — God is in this person's life. You can, you must try to seek God in every human life." For me, this was the most moving part of the lengthy interview.

The most common summary of Ignatian spirituality is the phrase "finding God in all things." Pope Francis reminds us that this means encountering God in all *people*. It makes sense, but it is a great challenge. It may be easy to find God in all people when they are people you like—or easier still when they like you—or when people present you with a pleasant exterior. It is easy to find God in a loving spouse, a gentle parent, a helpful neighbor, or a devoted child.

But what happens when the person is not so loving? Francis answers: God is in every person, no matter how difficult it may seem to find God there. I ask you to reread that beautiful quote: "Even if a life of a person has been a disaster, even if it has been destroyed by vices, drugs, or anything else—God is in this person's life. You can, you must try to seek God in every human life."

Because God is waiting for you there.

For Reflection

1. In whom do you encounter God most easily?
2. In whom is encountering God difficult?
3. Can you seek God in a person whose life seems to be a "disaster"?

"PRAYER FOR ME IS ALWAYS
A PRAYER FULL OF MEMORY,
OF RECOLLECTION."

Memory is an underappreciated part of the spiritual life. And rarely is it highlighted so much as it is in *A Big Heart Open to God*.

Many things can happen during private prayer—when you close your eyes and open yourself to God. Whether meditating on Scripture, praying during a Mass, or walking around in nature (not with your eyes closed!), you may experience all sorts of interior movements.

Emotions are common; you might feel sadness or joy while reading a certain Scripture passage. *Desires* are also common experiences in prayer; you could feel a longing to lead a holier life while listening to a sermon or homily. *Insights* may arise—something may suddenly seem clear, a solution to a vexing problem may dawn on you. Also, more general *feelings,* such as peace, or calm, or contentment, may also arise.

In each of these experiences, God is speaking with you.

But *memories* are a particularly underappreciated fruit of prayer. Sometimes when we pray we may be reminded of a warm memory, from, say, childhood. This may be a way that God can console you during a difficult time: when you feel alone or abandoned, God might raise up a memory as if to say, "Remember that I was with you then. And I am with you now." Or when you feel lonely, you might be reminded of a time with a close friend, and think, "I forgot about her friendship," and feel buoyed up.

A few months ago, I was praying about my Jesuit vocation. Suddenly, I was reminded of a moment from childhood that was suffused with joy. And I could almost feel the same joy as I prayed. I connected it instantly to my Jesuit vocation, and I seemed to see, in an instant, how much joy my Jesuit vocation had brought me. All this from a simple memory in prayer.

Memories that are not so pleasant can also arise—painful memories of loss or frustration or death. God may want to bring those up in prayer to allow you to look at them honestly, to speak about them with someone, or simply to heal them.

As the pope reminds us, when something comes up in prayer from your memory, pay attention. And ask yourself: What might God want to say to me here?

For Reflection

1. Think of a consoling time in your life when God felt especially present.

2. Rest in that moment.
3. Now thank God for that moment.

As Pope Francis said, God is to be found in every person. This means that God dwells within you, desires a relationship with you—and awaits you in prayer. May your meditation on the pope's words bring you closer to God.

James Martin, SJ, *is a Jesuit priest, editor at large at* America, *and author of several books, including* Jesus: A Pilgrimage *and* The Jesuit Guide to (Almost) Everything.